HE LEFT, GOD STAYED

HE LEFT, GOD STAYED

FROM REJECTION TO WHOLENESS
THROUGH GOD'S LOVE

Annalee Davis

Trilogy Christian Publishers
A Wholly Owned Subsidary of Trinity Broadcasting Network

2442 Michelle Drive
Tustin, CA 92780

For information, address Trilogy Christian Publishing

Rights Department, 2442 Michelle Drive, Tustin, CA 92780.

Trilogy Christian Publishing/ TBN and colophon are trademarks of Trinity Broadcasting Network.

For information about special discounts for bulk purchases, please contact Trilogy Christian Publishing.

Manufactured in the United States of America

10 9 8 7 6 5 4 3 2 1

Library of Congress Cataloging-in-Publication Data is available.

ISBN#: 978-1-64088-131-0

E-ISBN#: 978-1-64088-132-7

This book is dedicated to my mother, who modeled God's un-conditional love. She loved the Lord, her children, grandchildren and great-grandchildren with all her heart.

ACKNOWLEDGEMENTS

Thank you to my Heavenly Father for His unending and unfailing love. Thank you to my Lord and Savior, Jesus Christ, for coming into my heart at such a young age that I don't remember living a day of my life without Him. Thank you to the Holy Spirit for filling, guiding, comforting, inspiring and empowering me to be all I was created to be.

Thank you to my sons, Larry and Ryan, for their love and support and with their wonderful wives Jennifer and Lisa, respectively, have brought me seven reasons for incredible joy: Adrienne, Kaelyn, Anna, Chloe, Trinity, Declan and Kate. To my loving husband, Joel, for his support and encouragement, for listening and never judging my anxious moments. And thank you to my big Italian family and especially my brother and sister for their love and support.

Thank you to Eloise and Kathi for their friendship, love and prayer support over the years. Thank you to my prayer partners, especially Helene, Susan K. and Susan C.

Thank you to Frances Gregory Pasch, my Christian writer's group leader, for her undying encouragement and for opening her home for these many years to aspiring writers. To all the women of Hawke Point Writer's Group, thank you for your critiquing and for your friendship. You all hold a special place in my heart.

Thank you to Marlene Bagnull, who over these many years has worked tirelessly to direct the Greater Philadelphia and Colorado Christian Writer's Conferences, and who also opened her home to many of us who were in need of guidance and critiquing as we wrote our books.

Thank you to the whole production team at Trilogy Publishing. To Mark Mingle, Account Executive, for convincing me I had a story that needed to be heard, for reminding me that storing my book in my computer, wasn't helping anyone. Thank you to Nick Anderson, Project Manager for your help and expertise.

ENDORSEMENTS

Vulnerable and honest, *He Left, God Stayed,* is a touching and inspiring read that lifts the reader's heart from brokenness and loss to the assurance of God's loving presence. Annalee Davis, in the sharing of her story, reaches into God's Word and leaves readers standing firmly on the promises of God.

—Cindy Lambert, co-author of *Unplanned*

To move from betrayal and depression to hope and then to recovery and restoration is an age-old human story. Yet, my friend Annalee finds a way to tell hers in such a way that the reader is drawn in to feel the pain and despair, and, finally, invited to celebrate the restoring "of the years the locust has eaten" (see Joel 2:25). Each person who reads this moving book will benefit from discovering how to handle relationships that let us down, disappoint us or turn destructive. Annalee's personal interpretation of Psalm 55:12-14 is both gut-wrenching and, at the same time, life-giving. Thank you, Annalee, for your vulnerability and for your courage to write your story of freedom.

—Dr. Karl Eastlack, District Superintendent
for the *Northeast District of the Wesleyan Church*

Many of us have gone through the pain of rejection, whether by a spouse, a family member, or a friend. When we are at the bottom of the pit, we have nowhere to turn but to the Lord. In *He Left, God Stayed*, Annalee Davis tells her story of going through a devastating divorce. This book tells of her journey back to wholeness. It includes "Insights to Grow By," prayers, and relevant Scripture references. She learned to forgive those who wronged her and found complete restoration by leaning solely on the Lord.

—Susan Titus Osborn, author of over 30 books

Annalee's story is a beautiful and powerful testimony of God's grace and goodness in the midst of pain. It has a familiar sound that we hear in the stories of Scripture. Joseph overcame the pain of his brothers' betrayal and rose to a place of honor. Esther become queen and rescued her people in spite of the many oppositions. Annalee's engaging way of writing her vivid memories draws us into her story and into God's love and healing.

—**Anita Eastlack,** Executive Director –*Church Multiplication & Discipleship*, The Wesleyan Church

We don't learn to submit to the Lord until things are happening that we don't agree with. Until that happens, we just live in agreement! Annalee transparently shares her sorrows, suffering, and submission thru incredible losses during her life's story. But God's faithfulness came bursting through. She invites you to take a journey with her when, "*He Left, but God Stayed,*" faithful. All of us can relate to loss. Few of us experience it to this extreme. You will sense, "If God could bring her through all that, He can take me through anything!" Her story continues. Yours will too. This is a tribute to our Heavenly Husbandman, Who does all things well.

—**Len Meyers,** Pastor, Evangelist, President, *NewLifeChristianFellowshipInternational.net* and lifelong friend to the author

Annalee writes in a way that draws you into her story with moving dialog and a great choice of scriptures. She also includes unique "Insights to Grow By" and a prayer with each chapter that give the readers suggestions that may help them in their own lives. Her journey will tug at your heart and bring tears to your eyes as you follow her struggles. Throughout, Annalee incorporates a thread of God's faithfulness. Though He never left her, it often seemed He didn't hear her prayers. By His grace, she not only survived, but thrived!

—**Frances Gregory Pasch,** Poet and Devotional Writer

Annalee Davis shares her journey from betrayal and abandonment to forgiveness and restoration. Her insights are Scripture-based, and the truth of God's unfailing love and abundant grace come shining through. You will find hope and encouragement in the pages of *He Left, God Stayed*.

—**Marlene Bagnull,** Author, Director of the
Colorado and Greater Philadelphia Writers Conferences

With candor and discernment, Annalee recounts her journey from brokenness to wholeness. Walk alongside her and marvel over God's faithfulness. As she says, His love is greater than our pain, and He lovingly takes the shattered pieces of our lives and refashions them into something beautiful and holy. Each segment of her journey is capped with scriptural insights and a sample prayer, which enable readers to move forward in their journey to spiritual wholeness. Thank you, Annalee, for showing us how to leave heartbreak, shame, anger, and self-pity behind us as we embrace forgiveness, self-worth, and victory in Jesus Christ.

—**Denise K. Loock,** Author of *Open Your Hymnal*
and *Open Your Hymnal Again* devotional collections

TABLE OF CONTENTS

INTRODUCTION

Hello, friends! I'm so grateful you picked up this book. It is an answer to my prayers. You are soon to read about what I believe were the darkest hours of my life. During those years, my prayer was: "Lord, don't let this be for nothing! Don't let it be just for me! Let me use these experiences to bring hope to others in their pain!" The Lord has answered those prayers by giving me the opportunity to write my story.

As I've shared my life experiences over the years, some have said to me, "I never had *that kind* of pain or *that much* pain in my life!" —as if to say that my pain is somehow worse than their own. My question to them has been, "Have you had *any* pain in your life?" Of course, the answer is always, "Yes!" I remind them that pain is pain. We can't measure the depths of another's pain by their level of loss. We can only measure it by recognizing that we all suffer the same things while we are in pain. We all experience the same emotions and thoughts. We sense rejection, betrayal, abandonment, fear, anxiety, hopelessness, and helplessness. We ask ourselves questions like, "What will happen next?" "Will this pain *ever* end? When will this end?" "Did I do something to *deserve* this?" and, "Is God *punishing* me?"

Our greatest example of suffering is Jesus Christ. Jesus knew pain. I love the verse in Hebrews 4:15 in the King James Version. It reads: "For we have not an high priest which cannot be touched with the *feeling* of our infirmities; but was in all points tempted like as we are, yet without sin." Jesus knew suffering, just like we do. He felt abandoned by the disciples, rejected as the Messiah, betrayed by His followers, and anguished as He surrendered His will to the will of His Father in the Garden of Gethsemane and crucifixion on the cross. Isaiah 53:3 says:"He was despised and rejected by men, a man of sorrows, and familiar with suffering." And He knew loss and grief. When Lazarus died, Jesus cried. As both God and man, He knew what human emotions felt like and was familiar with what we go through in this life. Yet, He did it without sinning. Without turning away from God in His pain.

Don't think for one moment that God doesn't see and understand our pain! He does. But He also loves us in our pain. His love is greater than our pain! While we are in distress, we may not sense the love of God because our emotions are screaming at us. But as we lean into the pain, allow ourselves to feel what we need to feel, follow Jesus, call on the Holy Spirit, place our trust in our Heavenly Father, and allow Him into the deep places of our hearts, His love brings hope and healing. There is no experience, no situation, no circumstance, no loss, no disappointment that is beyond God's love to redeem. He can make our deepest hurt become a beacon of light in the darkness of another's soul.

I hope that as you read this book, you will see and understand that God never abandons us in our pain. He comes to us, surrounds us with His unfailing and unending love, and gives us peace in the midst of the storms of life. There is always hope in God! He is able to do things we can't do, work by the Holy Spirit in ways we can't, bring favor to us in our rejection, and cause others to be a blessing to us when we thought we were alone. There will be light at the end of the tunnel as we walk with Him—step by step—in the embrace of His loving arms.

This is a story of victory. It is a story of pain—but also of healing and wholeness. The Word of God speaks truth to us about who we are in Christ, how much He loves us, why we can have hope in every situation, and reaches into the depths of our wounded souls to speak new life. We are transformed by God's Word. It changes our minds and makes us new creations. So, I have included many Scripture verses in this book. The Bible is our foundation for living. When we eat and digest His Word, God makes the rough ways smooth and the crooked ways straight. He creates streams in the desert of our barren souls. I never imagined what the Lord would bring out of my suffering, but He saw a woman who, by His grace, would become who she was created to be. And it was His Word that brought me to that place.

It is my prayer that you will be encouraged, blessed, inspired, and renewed in your faith as you read this book. The events I share are from my perspective and memory. Along with a portion of my personal story, I share what I learned through each experience, and include a prayer at the end of each chapter that you can pray—especially if you aren't able to articulate your own prayers because of your pain. I've also included two appendices for you to return to when you need reinforcements. One with verses of comfort and encouragement from the Psalms—the other with assurances of God's love from both the Old and New Testaments.

And I hope you will share this book with someone who is suffering. Someone who is in a situation that seems hopeless. Someone who doesn't yet know the love of God and how great it is. And someone who thinks their life is over because of the rejection they have experienced. Let them know that God's love is greater than our pain. And my suffering will have been redeemed.

Abiding in His Amazing Love,

Annalee Davis

THE TRUTH HURTS

"He searches the sources of the rivers, and
brings hidden things to light."

—Job 28:11

Our church was reeling from the news, devastated that their pastor could leave his wife of twenty years and just disappear. He didn't just leave me. He left *all* of us. What about all those sermons on allowing God's love to build a strong marriage relationship? What about the fellowship enjoyed at church and family events? What about being faithful until death do us part? He had officiated wedding ceremonies for many people in the past twenty years of pastoring churches. If anyone knew the ins and outs of marriage, it was Larry.

While the people in the pew were rocked by my husband's sudden decision, in my dark, lonely hours the "what ifs" marched through my mind until I had to quote scripture out loud in order to make them stop.

Was Larry cheating on me? Is she a member of our church?

Did I ignore his discontent?

Who was he talking to right now about all of this?

What would our children do?

When I was home, all I could think about was Larry. When I was at church, friends and family assured me they were praying for me and my family. I was tempted to leave, but knew I needed their love and support. Staying offered my sons something familiar and the stability they needed.

In the meantime, Larry had moved out of our home in January and, not long after, moved into a large Victorian house with a wrap-around porch. He told me he was renting a room there. I couldn't imagine what possessed him to leave his friends, his family, his pastorate, and his faith to go off and rent a room in another town. It seemed to be a "bachelor's pad," and I secretly hoped he'd come to his senses after having to do his own laundry, cook his own meals, and "do life" without me there to help him.

Thankfully, I worked outside the home and church at a real estate office only fifteen minutes from my home. My job was a safe territory, a place where I could concentrate on something besides the empty place beside me in bed each morning. My friends were supportive after Larry left, but thankfully, they were not nosy. I was free to talk or free to hide in the ever-increasing mound of work. In fact, work was the one place I never expected the bombshell to fall.

As the work increased, so did my anxiety. The past few days had been filled with last-minute preparations for a trip to Texas the following week. *Finally, I've found a way to finish my bachelor's degree.* Southwestern Assemblies of God University in Waxahachie took all my credits from twenty-three years prior at Central Bible College and accepted me into their Adult Continuing Education Program. I could finish my education from my dining room table and still hold on to my secretarial job. The pressure built, but so did my excitement as I looked forward to a future filled with God's goodness.

CHAPTER 1: THE TRUTH HURTS

Then came that fateful day in July. It had started out as any other hot and humid day in New Jersey. But it would be etched in my memory forever. After following my daily routine of devotions, walking around my neighborhood for exercise, and eating breakfast, I dressed and left for work. I was running late.

When I arrived at work, walking through the back entrance to the office, I felt the uneasiness in the air. A stressful atmosphere wasn't unusual, with deals falling through and competition between agents abundant. However, on that day, the tension was palpable.

The morning hours included the usual phone calls, typing, and meeting the urgent—always urgent—needs of the agents. After lunch, I returned to my corner of the large office filled with desks and office equipment. A poster with the scene of a beautiful waterfall hung on the wall to my left. It read, "The prayers go up, the blessings come down." I trusted those words were true. It had been difficult since Larry had left. It had been more than six months of questions, emotional ups and downs, prayers—and waiting.

Allison, the office manager, was a dear Christian friend of mine. Her office was directly behind my desk. It had glass walls, and I could see clearly into her space. Often, in the bustle of the work day, I would turn around and talk to her through the open door.

Allison was connected to the surrounding communities and, as a high-producing realtor, she made it a point to attend parties of our real estate clients and loved to network with people. A couple of the agents in our office were gay, and Allison was often included in their party invitations.

This particular day, I noticed she sat at her desk, nervously shifting papers. I knew that something was wrong. Something had disturbed her spirit, but I didn't know what— and I hesitated to ask. Finally, she spoke up. I never expected the bomb that was about to fall.

"There was a party at Raymond's house on Saturday night," Allison began. Raymond was one of our real estate clients who had recently purchased the Victorian house where Larry now lived.

"Well, the porch collapsed in the middle of the party. You'll probably see the story in the newspaper. Raymond got drunk and began spouting to the crowd. He announced, 'I'm gay, and Larry is my lover.'"

"What did you say?" I asked, as I slowly turned to face Allison.

"Larry is gay," she repeated softly.

The words shocked me. I couldn't believe what I was hearing. I quickly drew a breath, holding it for a few seconds before I could exhale. I felt my heart pounding, and tears filled my eyes. My body began to tremble. My lunch churned in my stomach. I felt like I would vomit. I stared at Allison in disbelief. The weight of the pain of the past seven months came crashing down on me. My face must have revealed the aching in my heart.

Before Allison could say another word, I asked, "Can I go into the back room and make a phone call?"

She nodded in response. I grabbed my pocket-sized phone book from my purse. As I left the room, I heard Allison's sigh of relief. She later told me that she and one of the gay agents had felt they needed to tell me the truth about Larry and end the deception I had lived with. When Raymond made his announcement at the party, Allison felt it was time.

I forced my body to move down the hall to the back room where private meetings and conferences were held. My legs felt heavier than normal, my breathing was shallow, my heart pounded. Peeking through the partially open door to be sure I would be alone, I entered and sat down at the table.

With hands trembling, I picked up the phone and dialed Larry's mother. She and I had always had a good relationship. In fact, she had visited us the past June. At first, she stayed with Larry and Raymond, who I thought was just a roommate at the time. But after she slipped on the stairs and twisted her ankle, she came to stay with me for the remainder of her visit. I remember the two of us kneeling beside the bed that Larry and I once shared. On opposite sides of the bed, we reached out our hands to each other to pray. We sobbed and sobbed. But there was never any mention of Larry being gay.

My mother-in-law answered the call.

"Hello."

I skipped a greeting.

"Mom, is it true? Is Larry gay?" I asked.

"Yes, he says he's gay now," she said through her tears.

"Why didn't you tell me?"

"I couldn't. He wanted to tell you himself."

"He wanted to tell me! When was that going to be? I just found out from my office manager!"

I could hear her crying. I cried with her.

We had only talked for a few moments when we were interrupted by a knock on the door. An agent asked to use the room.

"I'll call back. I need to go," I abruptly told my mother-in-law. I hung up the phone, wiped my tears and left the room.

Shocked and confused, I walked back to my desk and asked Allison if I could go home early. She nodded.

I don't know how I drove home. My body was shaking again by the time I walked in the front door. As I slowly crept up the stairs to my bedroom, all I could think to do was to call my counselor, Anne.

As I dialed her number, I felt anger rising in my emotions. By the time she answered, I yelled in a high-pitched voice, "I just found out Larry is gay!"

She replied calmly, "It's shocking, isn't it?"

By the tone of her voice, I knew she had already figured out the dark secret from what I'd shared in our counseling sessions.

Suddenly I felt like the whole world knew about Larry's new gay life but me. I understood why Bob, a gay agent at the desk next to mine, came into the office and made negative remarks about Larry. The gay community didn't look favorably on what he had done.

The pieces of the puzzle started to fit together. I flashed back to my brother's wedding at the beginning of July. One of my cousins came up to me and told me I was a "beautiful woman." What had seemed strange at the time began to make sense. He knew Larry was gay, and he was trying to comfort me. People were discovering why Larry left, while I remained in the dark.

I hung up the phone and tried to figure out how I was going to tell our sons. I decided it was Larry's responsibility to tell them, not mine.

Then I called my mother. "I just found out that Larry is gay!" The words tumbled out of my mouth like I was a child refusing bitter-tasting food.

"Oh, my God! Oh, my God!" I could hear my mother crying. Then she began to pray in an unknown language, pouring her heart out to God for the daughter she loved and her family.

After a few minutes of crying and praying, I told her I would call back later. My sons would be home soon, and I didn't want them to see me with big red, puffy eyes. I needed to get control of myself and figure out what to do next. For the first time in all the confusion of the past year, I began to feel a sense of relief in knowing the truth.

CHAPTER 1: THE TRUTH HURTS

What had been hidden was brought to light.

I went through the evening without saying a word to my sons. That night, I crawled into my bed after my sons went to sleep. My body felt as if it weighed a thousand pounds. Lying on my stomach, I put my arms under my pillow and lowered my face into the cushion. I don't know how long I screamed. My heart was breaking. My chest heaved and ached as I drew each breath. That night, everything I had believed about our twenty-year marriage, and what I thought we had in our relationship, died. There was nothing left but pain.

****

INSIGHTS TO GROW BY

"If an enemy were insulting me, I could endure it; if a foe were raising himself against me, I could hide from him. But it is you...my companion, my close friend, with whom I once enjoyed sweet fellowship as we walked with the throng at the house of God" (Psalm 55:12-14).

Betrayal is a terrible thing. As we go through life, there will be times that we feel betrayed by someone. A friend, a co-worker, or a relative may betray us in some way. When it happens, our trust is shaken and our belief in that person is torn from us by their act of betrayal. We are shocked to discover that someone we thought was interested in our well-being has turned on us to inflict a wound. Since trust is the foundation for any healthy relationship, when it is shattered, it takes time for the one who was betrayed to trust again.

Jesus was betrayed during His earthly life. The betrayal came from Judas, one of His disciples. Judas had followed Jesus around Israel, watched Him perform miracles, listened to His profound teaching, and learned what it meant to be a part of the kingdom of God. They were friends. Yet, Judas chose to betray Jesus. Betrayal was inescapable even for the Son of God. Fallen human nature makes people turn their backs on those who trust them as friends.

I believe there are different levels of betrayal. Some wounds go deeper than others. Some relationships, such as the one between a parent and child, are vital to our survival. When a parent betrays a child, it is monumental in its lifelong effects. It takes years for the wounded child to heal. As an adult, the person may struggle with the ability to trust enough to have normal, loving relationships. Sadly, there are those who never recover from the parent-child wound. They move through their entire lives trying to survive, never thriving.

One of the deepest levels of betrayal is betrayal from a spouse. Not only is trust the foundation for all healthy interpersonal relationships, it is the very basis for marriage. There can be no meaningful marriage relationship without trust at its core. The vows are shared, the promises are made, and both bride and groom expect their beloved to keep what they have committed to one another. Unfaithfulness violates everything that was ever precious between a husband and wife.

When betrayal makes its way into the deep places of this relationship, the results are devastating. When I learned about Larry's betrayal, I could identify with the words of Psalm 55. David was grieving. "My heart is in anguish within me; and terrors of death assail me. Fear and trembling have beset me; horror has overwhelmed me" (v.4, 5).

We expect an enemy to harm us. We expect those who hate us to rise up against us. But when our enemy turns out to be our companion, our close friend, our lover-- it is horrible. When it is the one we shared our bed with, the one whom we bared our souls to, and the one in whose care we placed our fragile hearts---it makes us tremble. When our spouse was a fellow Christian and we had sweet fellowship and worshiped God together--- it is crushing.

But it is not beyond the scope of God's love for us. God's love is greater than our pain. His love is what will bring us through the devastation to a better place. Psalm 94 assures us of this truth. "Unless the Lord had given me help, I would soon have dwelt in the silence of death. When I said, 'My foot is slipping,' your love, O Lord, supported me. When anxiety was great within me, your consolation brought joy to my soul" (v. 17-19).

Unfortunately, if you live long enough, someone will betray you. I hope it isn't your spouse. But if it is, God will support you with His everlasting arms. He will not let the wound kill you. You may want to die, but God's love will sustain you in your grief. When you feel like you are not going to survive, God will give you consolation. The Holy Spirit will bring comfort. As you allow the tears to flow, the Lord will be the One who brings peace—and eventually joy—to your soul. You can trust Him in times of betrayal. Even if you don't feel you can trust anyone else, Jesus is always trustworthy. He is the Friend who will never betray you.

****

PRAYER

Lord, my whole being is aching with grief and disbelief. I feel like my heart will break beyond repair. Your Word says Your love will support me in my pain. I desperately want to believe that You are bigger than all of this and You won't allow it to kill me. Help me to trust You when I am unable to trust others. Assure me of Your presence in my sorrow. I ask this in Your name, Amen.

A CRACKED FOUNDATION

"Before I formed you in the womb I knew you, before you were born I set you apart."
—Jeremiah 1:5

While five hundred people sat in church wondering what happened, I rehearsed the events of my life in an attempt to determine why I had made the choices I'd made.

The most important decision of my life came on Mother's Day, May 8, 1955, when I gave my heart to Jesus. My mother sat next to me in old Ebenezer Assembly of God Church in Elizabeth, New Jersey. Noticing the tears streaming down my five-year-old cheeks during the altar call, she asked me if I wanted to accept Jesus into my heart. I nodded. I had the overwhelming sense that I was a sinner and I needed Jesus as my Savior. My mother took my hand and led me to the altar. We knelt down and she prayed a prayer that I repeated:

"Dear Jesus, please forgive me of my sin. I ask You to come into my heart and be Lord of my life. I want to live for You and be with You forever in heaven. Amen."

I remember that my mother embraced me and smiled at me

with her big, blue eyes. She whispered into my ear, "Thank you for the best Mother's Day gift." I looked into the face of the woman I loved as she dried my tears with her handkerchief. Her dark hair fell in waves around her olive complexion. To me she was the most beautiful woman in the world. I hugged her tightly.

The next day, I ran up the stairs to the second floor of our two-family home and barged through the door.

"Auntie Phyllis, Auntie Phyllis!"

"What is it?"

"Yesterday I got saved. I gave my heart to Jesus!"

My mother followed closely behind, and after my announcement she said, "Well, honey, you are half-saved." *Half-saved? Does that mean I'm not going to heaven?* Her words confused me. I wanted to be sure my sins were forgiven and I was going to heaven.

My mother later shared with me that she told me I was only half-saved so I would continue to seek the Lord in my life. She didn't want me to be satisfied with a one-time experience. And I wasn't.

By the age of nine, I was at the same church altar experiencing the gift of tongues. Once again, my mother was beside me, encouraging me to speak out the language God was giving me. With trembling lips, I spoke out words I'd never heard before in praise and adoration to the Lord. The warmth and peace of His presence was so real and comforting to me.

I continued to love Jesus and grow in my relationship with the Lover of my soul. I enjoyed going to church and learning about Him and reading the Bible. Often, I sat on my bed and read my favorite Bible passages, John 3:16 and Psalm 8. I especially loved verses 2 and 4 of the Psalm: "From the lips of children and infants you have ordained praise." "What is man that you are mindful of him?" I read those words over and over. I questioned God. Why do You love me?

CHAPTER 2: A CRACKED FOUNDATION

Why would You even take the time to think about me? Yet, my faith, even as a child, affirmed to me that the words of Psalm 8 were true. Knowing that God loved me, and that He was thinking about me, warmed my heart and gave me a sense of significance in the world.

Church activities filled my growing years. Sunday morning and evening services, Vacation Bible School, prayer meetings, camp meetings, young girls' clubs, and missions conventions helped my faith to grow and most likely kept me out of trouble. Almost everyone in my large, Italian family went to the church we attended. I saw cousins, aunts, uncles, grandparents, and many of my mother's fifty-one first cousins at church events.

Holidays were especially fun. We gathered at my grandparents' house and enjoyed mounds of hand-made raviolis smothered in tomato sauce made from home-grown tomatoes. My grandfather's garden was fabulous. Besides tomatoes and basil, he grew a variety of vegetables and nurtured a couple of fig trees. In late summer, I stood with family and picked fresh, plump figs off the trees, savoring every mouthful. To this day, every time I eat a fresh fig, my senses are transported back to my grandfather's garden.

My grandmother always prayed for our meals in Italian, and I loved the graceful words that flowed from her lips. Nana, as we called her, was a beautiful, dignified woman from the region of Naples, Italy. She and her six sisters immigrated to the United States early in the twentieth century. She came to know Jesus personally through a physical healing and never looked back. She abandoned her former religious life of fear and superstition, rearing her family of five daughters in the same church we attended as a family.

Although my relationship with my mother's family was close, my relationship with my father and his family was not. My grandmother refused to hold me as an infant, because I "made her a grandmother." My father frightened me. He emulated Jackie Gleason on the TV series "The Honeymooners" and referred to himself as "the king of the castle." He yelled a lot. He would come into the house at the end of his workday, and if dinner wasn't hot and on the table, my mother would get his unwarranted anger. She was demeaned by him with remarks like, "How stupid can you be?"

I learned from my father's words that women were deficient. They couldn't make decisions for themselves. They were a step below men in intelligence. Women were good for having children and running a household. And, at the time, these ideas were reinforced by my church.

The denomination in which I grew up has ordained women since 1925. However, in my home church women were limited in what they were allowed to do in ministry. They could teach Sunday School and sing in the choir. They could clean the church and conduct Vacation Bible School. But the men were in control, and the women knew "their place." It didn't include leadership or positions of authority.

I never felt good enough for my father, and I knew why. I wasn't a boy. He desperately wanted a son. Three years after I was born, my sister was born. Then my mother had two miscarriages. One a girl, the last a boy.

I remember the night my father received the phone call from the hospital where my mother had prematurely delivered the baby boy. It was late and I was already asleep, but the ring of the phone startled me, so I was alert enough to hear the conversation. After a couple of "Uh-hmm"s, I heard my father cry.

"The baby died?" he asked the caller.

Another "Uh-hmmm." Then he hung up the phone and cried aloud, and his sobs echoed through the house. Tears fell from my eyes and dropped on to my pillow. As a nine-year-old, I was frightened by my father's tears, and I missed my mother.

Two years later, my mother gave birth, prematurely once again, but the baby boy survived. When he was released from the hospital, my sister and I hovered over his bassinet in my parents' bedroom like a hen over her chicks. Our family had waited for another child for eight years. And I finally had the brother that I desired and that my father longed for.

I'll never forget the day he was dedicated to the Lord at church. My sister and I sat in the congregation on the hard oak pews and watched as my parents carried my brother up to our pastor. He gently cradled the new life in his arms and said, "Just like Abraham, this is the promised son to these parents." With my hands neatly folded in my lap, I shifted in my seat, slid down slightly and lowered my head. I felt invisible.

When I was twenty-one years old, my father told me something that confirmed what I already knew deep in my heart. I don't remember why we were alone, just the two of us, that day in my parents' kitchen.

"I cried when you were born," my father said. Startled at his statement that came so unexpectedly while we stood there together preparing lunch, I tried to act calm. But my heart was racing, and I wouldn't look at him because I feared he would see the tears welling up in my eyes.

"Why?" I asked.

"Because you were a girl, and I wanted a boy."

A physical punch in the stomach would have been easier to cope with than the emotional stab to my heart. The wound was inflicted. I was the wrong gender for my father. I never felt cherished by him. I never heard "I'm proud of you." In my entire life, I only heard "I love you" twice---once was on his death bed. Throughout my life, I never sensed my father's approval.

When we were in a public venue, my father always introduced me as "his beautiful daughter." I would cringe as those words came out of his mouth. My little sister was never described the same way, and I could see the pain on her face as she was described as "my other daughter."

I learned early in life that my worth was in my appearance. I was told all through my growing years, by my mother and everyone in my family, that I was beautiful. I believed what I heard and was always concerned with my appearance. It carried into my teenage years, to the point that I wouldn't go out of the house without having the "right" look. My hair, clothes, and make-up all had to be in style. I learned to hide behind the facade of a pretty face and well-clothed, slim body. I became skilled at giving the appearance of confidence and poise. Under the mask was a very wounded child-- yearning to be healed.

****

INSIGHTS TO GROW BY

"Though my father and mother forsake me, the Lord will receive me" (Psalm 27:10).

The world is filled with stories of fractured lives that were built on cracked foundations. Even the Bible contains stories of damaged relationships between parents and children that brought pain and discord. Genesis 25 gives us the account of twins given to Isaac and Rebekah. Verse 28 reads: "Isaac…loved Esau, but Rebekah loved Jacob." This imbalance of love and acceptance caused years of jealousy, deceit, and separation.

When a foundation of love, acceptance, and approval are present in a child's life, as they grow they can make decisions based on a sense of their worth and value to those who love them. In the same way, when we are devalued, rejected, and left feeling unloved, our lives are often filled with fruitless attempts to fill the void left from a painful childhood.

CHAPTER 2: A CRACKED FOUNDATION

Dare I say that we all come out of childhood wounded? The wounds may be inflicted by family or those outside our home, but whatever the source, they are painful. As children, we believe we are responsible in some way for the wound. We think we must have done something to deserve the pain. The truth is, we are not responsible for the actions or words of those who have hurt us.

So many people, both in and out of the church community, have felt the pain of being physically or emotionally forsaken by one or both of their parents. Living in a Christian home does not protect us from experiencing the pain of rejection. Growing up in the church is not a guarantee of a childhood free of emotional suffering.

The only One we can count on to love us unconditionally is Jesus. The divine love of God is far greater than any human love can ever be. When everyone else abandons us, when we are rejected and despised, when we are abused and neglected, the Lord Jesus will receive us. Hebrews 13:5 reminds us: "Never will I leave you, never will I forsake you." These words are a promise from Almighty God—the God who knew us before we were formed in our mother's womb. It is this loving God who knows our pain and wants to heal the wounds of our childhood. The reality of our childhood pain is not too hard for God. "For nothing is impossible with God" (Luke 1:37).

* * * * * * *

PRAYER

Lord, I give You the pain of my childhood. Please heal the wounds I received. I ask You, by Your Spirit, to reach into the deep places of my heart and soul and bring wholeness. Help me to know that You are with me and will never leave me or forsake me. Give me a revelation of how much You love me. Receive me to Yourself, I pray. In Jesus' name, Amen.

BUILDING OUR LIVES

"Trust in the Lord with all your heart and lean not on your own understanding; in all your ways acknowledge him, and he will make your paths straight."
—Proverbs 3:5

As I entered my teen years, I sensed the Lord speaking to me about going into full-time ministry. There was a tugging at my heart that I couldn't ignore or resist. One Sunday evening during a missions convention at church, I went to the altar to pray.

Are you willing to go? There it was again—that still, small voice.

No, Lord. Don't ask me to leave my family and go to some foreign land.

Are you willing to go, my child?

I cried. Beads of sweat formed on my forehead and upper lip.

Why me? I don't want to go to Africa. In my youthful mind, going into ministry meant the possibility of going to Africa as a missionary.

I'm scared, Lord.

I wrestled with God for several more minutes. I didn't know what it would mean to say "yes" to this tugging on my heart. I did know that I wouldn't be able to choose my own way, my own path in life. I would choose to go where He wanted me to go and be what He wanted me to be.

Finally, I prayed, *Yes, Lord. I'll go where You want me to go. I'll do what You want me to do. I'll be what You want me to be.*

I was sixteen years old.

After I graduated high school, in the fall of 1967, my family packed our aqua Chrysler station wagon and ventured out to Springfield, Missouri, where I had been accepted to attend Central Bible College. It was hot and crowded in the back seat of the car with my younger sister and brother. There was no air-conditioning in those days.

I loved my family. During the trip, as I thought of being so far from them while I prepared for the ministry, I repeatedly choked back tears. But I was excited about going to college and the new life that was about to begin. The trip was long, and I was relieved when we arrived at the campus after two days of driving.

Stately oak trees, winding paths, and a warm Missouri breeze welcomed us as we drove onto the campus. My heart raced with anticipation as I walked up the stairs to the dorm. My father carried my trunk full of clothes, and the rest of the family lugged bags of toiletries and personal belongings up the three flights of stairs to my room. Bowie Hall was old and in need of remodeling. When I saw my room, my first impression was, *Oh, no! This is not what I expected.* It was small, and the bunk bed allowed just enough room for my roommate and me to get to our dressers. I tearfully said good-bye to my family and settled in to college life.

One day early into the semester, I noticed an announcement on one of the bulletin boards: "Come to the Music Building on Monday at 3:00 P.M. to try out for Revivaltime Choir." I had only briefly heard about the radio choir that sang every Sunday evening on 600 national and international radio stations. I decided to try out.

Two days later, I screeched and clapped my hands as I read my name on the list of sopranos who were selected to sing in the choir. My roommate, a petite brunette with an alto voice, was also chosen.

I called my mother, "I've been accepted into Revivaltime. I can't believe it. I'll be singing on the radio every Sunday night and taking national tours with the choir."

"Oh, sweetheart. I'm so excited for you. I'll listen every Sunday night." My mother kept her promise.

And that's where I met Larry. He was a Michigander with a smooth, baritone voice. He was tall, with light hair and blue eyes. Blue eyes like my mother. He had been accepted into the choir the year before I arrived. Along with fifty other students, we sang and toured through the fall months of my freshman year. I was disappointed when he didn't return to school after the Christmas holiday break.

One night during the spring semester, I answered the hall phone in my dorm. It was Larry, calling his girlfriend. I recognized his voice immediately.

"Hi, Larry," I said. "We've missed you."

"I'll be back in the fall," he assured me. I was excited at the thought of seeing him again. I considered him a friend and was happy to see him back on campus when he returned to Springfield.

By my sophomore year Larry and I were dating. I liked his gentle manner and sense of humor. He respected me and treated me well. He sent me cards and flowers, and took me to the nicer restaurants in the rolling hills of the Ozarks. I was impressed that he treated me so royally on a student's budget. He worked hard as an orderly as he pursued his degree in Biblical Studies.

One night, as we walked down one of the winding pathways on campus, we stopped to talk.

Larry began, "I've been called to ministry, but I want you to know, I will never pastor a church."

"That's fine with me. I never want to be a pastor's wife," I replied.

It was settled. We were both called into ministry, but we wanted to decide where we would serve. Little did we know what the Lord had in store for us.

On June 21, 1969, very much in love, Larry and I were married in the new building that Ebenezer Church (which changed its name to Evangel Church in the move) had built in my hometown. It was a beautiful wedding ceremony. My chaplain uncle, and the pastor who officiated at my parents' wedding and dedicated me to the Lord, heard us make vows to love each other until death. After a honeymoon in the Bahamas, we settled into married life.

Returning to Springfield in September, Larry continued his studies, but I dropped out of college to help support us while he finished his education. I worked as a seamstress until Larry graduated. After graduation, we packed our car and headed back to New Jersey.

Our first ministry position was at my home church. Larry served as the first salaried youth pastor. A year later, we were called to pastor a small mission church in a well-to-do town in central New Jersey. So much for our plans of what we would not do in the ministry!

Excited about our new ministry opportunity, we diligently searched for an apartment, trying to find a place that would accommodate my growing abdomen. I was five months pregnant with our first child, and we wanted a place on the first floor. Scheduled to move on a Saturday, my friend Eloise came to our apartment to help me pack. It was a Thursday evening.

CHAPTER 3: BUILDING OUR LIVES

"So, where are you moving to?" she asked.

"We don't know yet," I responded. Feeling embarrassed, I kept my head down while I packed. After a few moments, I looked up at her.

"You don't know? Why are we packing?" She looked at me curiously, tilting her head as she spoke.

"Because we are moving on Saturday. I don't know where we're going, but I'm trusting that the Lord will provide a place for us."

I could see the confusion in her eyes. I knew it sounded strange, but I had no other concrete answer to give her. I expressed my appreciation to her that she had come to help, and we continued packing.

On Friday, Larry and I went once again to the town where we would pastor and looked for an apartment. We found nothing.

Discouraged, Larry prayed aloud, "Lord, we need a place to live. Please provide for us."

As we drove out of town, Larry stopped the car to ask a man walking down the street where there might be an apartment complex for us to rent an apartment. He gave us directions to a place he thought might have a vacancy.

Driving longer than we expected, we soon realized we were lost. We saw a different apartment complex than the one the stranger had directed us to, and we drove up to the manager's office. We approached a man sitting at his desk

"Do you have any apartments available?" Larry asked.

"What are you looking for?" the man inquired.

"We need a one-bedroom on the first floor," Larry answered.

"We just finished painting one."

"When can we move in?"

"Tomorrow morning."

It was right within our price range.

The Lord was teaching me a lesson on His faithfulness. I needed to remember that lesson many more times over the coming years.

Not long after we moved into our new apartment, our first son, Larry Jr., was born. My husband was with me for the entire labor and delivery. When the doctor placed our new baby on my chest immediately after he was born, we both stared in awe at the precious new life that had just come into our world.

"He's beautiful," I whispered, exhausted from giving birth.

"He has your dark coloring," Larry added.

He took my hand and looked into my eyes.

"I want you to know, you never have to go through this again, if you don't want to."

Two years and eight months later, our second son, Ryan, was born. He had light hair and blue eyes. Right after his birth, the nurse cradled him in one arm and with her other hand, she pointed out the dimples in his cheeks. He looked just like his father. Our family was complete.

We continued to pastor over the years both in New Jersey and Michigan. Often, Larry and I sang together, blending the soprano and baritone voices that had brought us together during our college years. Larry was a good preacher and administrator. His compassion for people was evident, but he also became frustrated and irritated easily when dealing with parishioners. There were times when the pressure was enormous, and conflict robbed us of the joy of being in ministry.

CHAPTER 3: BUILDING OUR LIVES

I tried to be the perfect pastor's wife. I sang, played the piano and organ, kept the parsonage decorated and clean, taught Sunday School, entertained parishioners and guest speakers, made home-made meals with home-canned food, and earned extra income by making clothes and selling crafts.

But there was a void in my heart. Larry and I didn't pray togeth-er. We didn't share very often about the Lord or have devotions on a regular basis. We attended church, conferences, ministers' meetings and national conventions together. Yet, there was something missing. I longed for more in our relationship.

One day while living in Michigan, I took the car and went for a ride. We lived in the country, ten miles from the nearest town. As I passed corn field after corn field, I cried out to the Lord.

I'm not content. I don't know what to do. There's something lacking in our marriage relationship. I feel neglected and ignored sometimes, Lord. We don't pray together or have devotions. What should I do? When I approach Larry about my desires, he just gets angry.

The reply was almost audible.

"Don't look to your spouse for what only I can give you in your relationship with Me."

Okay. I get it. You are the One I need and You are the only One who can fill this void in my heart.

I took a deep breath and drove home with a new sense of peace.

The next morning, I awoke before anyone else and went to the couch in the living room, wrapping myself in the soft folds of an af-ghan my mother had crocheted and sent to us. I took a pad of paper and a pen and wrote as I felt prompted by the Lord:

ANOTHER DAY

Lord, bless this, another day
And with each work-filled hour
May I feel the warmth and strength
Of Your Holy Spirit's power.

Lord, bless this, another day
May it not slip idly past
But be used to build our home
On important things that last.

Lord, use me on this day
To be a shining light
To those whose lives are trapped
In sin's cold and darkest night.

I ask, dear Lord, today
That in whatever may befall
Your living face I'll see
And I'll recognize Your call.

For as each new day arrives
I long to know You more
So my life fulfills Your purpose
'Til I reach that golden shore.

Lord, bless this, another day
I commit it now to You
May Your perfect love and grace
Be seen in all I do.

CHAPTER 3: BUILDING OUR LIVES

As the years passed, we moved into other ministry positions. Finally, in the mid- 1980s, we were asked to pastor my home church in New Jersey. By that time the church had doubled in size. They had moved into a suburb of my hometown and into a new, Colonial-style building with Palladian windows and brass chandeliers. It was a beautiful facility, and each Sunday morning rays of sunlight shone through those windows, reminding me of God's loving-kindness in our lives. Our sons were teenagers by then, and we were all delighted to be back with family and old friends.

Living in apartments and parsonages was common in the ministry, but we wanted to own our own home. We searched for a house we could afford. One day, while driving aimlessly, looking for homes on the market, we stumbled on a development of new houses. *Could it be possible to own a new house?* We drove up to the office and went inside.

The young woman at the desk offered to show us the models already built and decorated.

We followed her into the Sycamore model home and I knew it was what I wanted.

My excitement built as I picked out the colors of carpet and flooring and decided what type of wood cabinets I wanted in the kitchen. Together, Larry and I chose cream-colored siding with blue shutters for the outside of our new home, in keeping with the Colonial style of homes in the area.

The day finally came when we closed on the house. Filled with excitement, Larry's hands shook as he opened the door and we all ran inside. Larry and Ryan ran from room to room, jumping and laughing. We were in our dream house. What fun I had decorating! I wallpapered and stenciled and made curtains to match the stencil design. Everything was carefully coordinated. It was all done with loving care. I wanted it to be a place of comfort, peace, and rest for our family.

What more could I ever want? A wonderful family, a new home, ministry in my home church with people who loved me, and a good salary. This is as good as it gets!

We felt a sense of stability and security in our new home and in our new place of ministry. But it wouldn't last for long.

****

INSIGHTS TO GROW BY

"In his heart a man plans his course, but the Lord determines his steps" (Proverbs 16:9).

Solomon, the wisest man who ever walked the earth, wrote these words. He lived long enough to know that we may plan our lives, but ultimately the Lord determines where we will go and what we will do.

Somehow, in my childish thinking, I believed that because I had come to the Lord at a young age and was following the call of God on my life, I would not experience some of the hardships that others faced. I believed that if I "followed all the rules" —live for Jesus, marry a Christian man, be active in ministry—my life would be insulated from terrible pain and suffering. It seemed so simple. Do this... don't do that...and you are guaranteed a great life! Legalism feels safe to many Christians. We believe that if we have a set of rules to follow, we won't go astray. If we walk in obedience, things will always go well for us. That kind of thinking is not biblical, nor is it in touch with reality. It also makes room for a judgmental spirit. It's easy to look at the lives of others and judge when they are experiencing pain or suffering. I thought that people, especially non-Christians, were experiencing painful lives because they were not following the "rules" for living that God gave us in His Word.

It is wonderful to have dreams and visions for our lives. Who would want to live without a dream for the future? But we can't plan our lives on faulty thinking or childish belief systems that tell us that as Christians we won't experience pain and suffering, that we are immune from tragedy or trauma, and that we are above what unbelievers go through.

We all expect the usual bumps and bruises of life, but never imagine that tragedy will strike at the very foundation of our lives, forcing us to reevaluate our beliefs about ourselves, God, and the world around us. When we give our lives to Jesus, He doesn't guarantee the absence of suffering. In fact, He tells us that we will have trouble in this world, but that by His power living in us, we can overcome the world. Jesus encouraged His disciples, "I have told you these things, so that in me you may have peace. In this world you will have trouble. But take heart! I have overcome the world" (John 16:33). And those words apply to us as His disciples.

It's important to make plans. But as children of God, we must give our plans over to the Lord and trust Him with our future. Whether we are in full-time ministry, teaching Sunday School, or singing in the choir, our lives have been purchased with Jesus' own blood, and we belong to Him alone.

As we learn to trust Him with our dreams and desires, He proves over and over again that He is worthy of our complete trust. He knew us when we were in our mother's wombs, and He knows what is best for us and those we love.

When we look back over our lives, we will be able to see the hand of God leading, guiding, and protecting us. We have no guarantee of a pain-free life. We do have a guarantee that God will be with us, and that He will bring us through the suffering.

* * * * * * *

PRAYER

Lord, help us to remember that we can make our plans, but that You are the One who determines the course of our lives. Help us to relinquish all our dreams to Your purposes and plan for us. Give us a vision for what You want for our lives. We ask for the faith to trust You with our desires as we surrender to Your will. In Jesus' name we pray, Amen.

CHAPTER FOUR

BURIED MEMORIES

"He reveals deep and hidden things; he knows what lies in darkness, and light dwells with him."
—Daniel 2:22

I found myself sitting in the winged chair in my living room, staring out through the lace curtains which gracefully draped the picture window. It had become a habit. I had been getting up with my sons at 6:30 a.m., sending them off to high school, and then sluggishly trying to make my way through the day. My body felt twice its weight. My thinking was clouded. I felt disoriented, distant from my own existence. A couple of times a week I walked aimlessly through a local discount clothing store. I browsed the merchandise as if I was looking for something I couldn't find. What was it? What was I searching for?

But lately, I felt drawn to sit in the chair, just staring. I wondered, *Could this be depression?* One day I sat in that cozy arm chair for two hours, completely unable to function. The sense of absolute isolation chilled the air. Tears filled my eyes. I desperately cried out to the Lord, "Please, God! I give You permission to change my life! I can't live like this anymore. What's wrong? This is not how I want to live!"

It wasn't long before that prayer was answered. Both Larry and I were struggling under the weight of the demands of the church. We were attending services twice on Sunday and on Wednesday evenings. Each month, there was a women's ministry meeting on Tuesday night. My sons went to youth group on Friday nights. And Larry was hosting seminars and workshops on Saturdays. At one point, I was going into the church office to help with secretarial work. The pressure was enormous. There were days when I was so exhausted, I had nothing left to give my sons when they came home from school.

I never said "no" to anything Larry asked of me. After all, we were in the ministry and we had to do whatever needed to be done. I was gifted in areas that enhanced our ministry, and I felt obligated to do whatever he asked. If I hesitated or resisted his requests, his response was, "Why are you doing this to me?"

Food was my comfort and escape. There were times when I ate until I was nauseous. I stuffed my feelings down with anything I could grab from the refrigerator. When I couldn't eat anymore, I bent over the toilet, held my aching stomach and tried to bring up what I had stuffed down. I later learned that I was acting bulimic.

One day, I began to black out while in the bathroom. My vision blurred and I felt like I was entering a dark tunnel. I sat on the floor until I came to my senses again and was able to get up and walk out of the room. I knew I was out of control. I couldn't endure the pressure of my life any longer.

To add to my personal problems, there was conflict and discontent among the leaders of the church. I remember Larry coming home one night after a church board meeting. The sessions always lasted until well after midnight. I awoke as he crawled into bed that night.

"How did the meeting go?"

"It was horrible."

CHAPTER 4: BURIED MEMORIES

"What happened?"

"The first half hour [one particular board member] railed at me over how the church isn't growing, and that it's my fault."

"Did anyone come to your defense?"

"No one. The rest sat there and just listened. I felt like I was being raped. I feel betrayed."

I thought his remark was strange. I felt sad and frightened that he would experience such negative emotions in the place where we felt called to minister. I didn't have an answer as to why things were not going well. Ministry was all we had known, and I couldn't imagine doing anything else in life.

It was a few weeks later when Larry came home one day from working out in the gym and asked me to come upstairs to our bedroom because he wanted to tell me something in private.

As we climbed the stairs, I could sense something was terribly wrong. The look on his face was one of shock and pain. His eyes were wide with disbelief and his voice was shaky as he spoke.

"While I was working out in the gym today, I began to have memories of sexual abuse during my childhood."

"Oh, God, Larry! That's horrible! What are you remembering?"

Larry shared with me the few pieces he had been able to put together of this tragic revelation. Eventually, he would remember eight years of childhood sexual abuse, beginning at the age of three. Most of it was violent.

There were days when I grieved for the little boy who was so brutally violated. I cried for the child who was destroyed by the sickness and perversion of others. There were days when we cried together and wondered why the memories were surfacing at that time. What was happening? What would it mean for our lives and our future?

I watched as Larry struggled to keep working and preaching. Over the next few months, I saw his demeanor slowly change. The person I saw as someone who never exhibited anger began to show signs of rage and rebellion against everything we valued. He withdrew from our family life and refused to be accountable to me or anyone else.

I encouraged Larry to find a counselor. He agreed that he needed someone to help him work through his pain. He didn't want a Christian counselor, so he found a man who described himself as "an agnostic Jew." That Larry didn't want a Christian counselor frightened me. I didn't understand why he wasn't moving towards the Lord for healing.

It only took a few months for Larry to make the decision to resign from the church. He announced to me without discussion between us that he would leave after the first of January. He said he couldn't go on in his position with what he was experiencing. I told him I understood. But I was terrified.

****

INSIGHTS TO GROW BY

"Listen to my cry, for I am in desperate need" (Psalm 142:6).

I gave the Lord permission to change my life, never imaging what that would mean for my future. The desperation I felt for something more and better was warranted. I wasn't functioning on the level of living a full and satisfying life. Depression ruled my emotions. I knew there had to be more for me. Jesus said, "I have come that they might have life, and that they might have it more abundantly" (John 10:10 KJV). I wanted that abundance.

Sometimes our discontent, and the resulting cry of desperation to God, opens the way for the Holy Spirit to come into our situation and bring about change. As I was growing up in church, my pastor often said, "The Holy Spirit is a gentleman." He was teaching us that God, by His Spirit, would not force Himself on us to make us change. He shared that we must invite the Spirit into our lives and desire for God to work in us and transform us by His power. That's the only way we would see significant and lasting change in our lives.

When we're ready, the Holy Spirit does bring about change. Not simply change for the sake of something different. Change for the sake of healing. We are restless and discontent because we are not free from the pain of the past. It still has a stranglehold on our lives, and we can't live up to our potential. The Spirit of God wants to bring us to a place of wholeness and liberty. He wants us to live without guilt from the past or fear of the future.

The Lord hears our cries and knows the longing of our hearts. He understands when we feel desperate for something new, something better. But He won't engineer the circumstances of our lives to allow for the changes unless we give Him permission. We must surrender our will to the will of God.

My prayer for change was heard by God, but His answer was not what I expected. It began with Larry's memories, but would continue with more pain and upheaval in our lives. I watched Larry change in ways that were frightening to me. Before long, the grief I felt for his lost childhood was overshadowed by anxiety. Our lives were changing, and we would never be the same. The future was uncertain, and I had nowhere to turn but to the Lord.

* * * * * * *

PRAYER

Jesus, You've promised to give us abundant life. We long for all the fullness of a life completely surrendered to You. Please don't allow our wounds to control us and deny us all that You have planned for us. We say "yes" to Your healing, transforming power, and we invite Your Spirit to dispel our discontent. In Your name we pray, Amen.

CHAPTER FIVE

"I WILL NOT LET YOU FALTER"

"'For I know the plans the plans I have for you,' declares the Lord, 'plans to prosper you and not to harm you, plans to give you hope and a future'."
—Jeremiah 29:11

Autumn is my favorite season. I especially love the fall in Lancaster County, Pennsylvania, in the middle of Amish country. The hills are riddled with orange, gold, and rust colored leaves, and farms are dotted with red barns and white silos. The fall of 1988 seemed especially beautiful. As we drove up to Willow Valley Retreat Center, bales of hay cradled pumpkins and potted mums. I loved being at the yearly women's retreat with my home church. For the past two years, I'd attended as the pastor's wife.

I arrived for the retreat on Friday night with friends who offered to drive me home early Sunday morning before the official end of the weekend retreat. They knew Larry planned to announce his resignation to our congregation. I appreciated their willingness to help me attend the retreat yet fulfill my obligation to stand at my husband's side while he resigned. The stress of ministry and family had caused physical and emotional exhaustion. I wanted to be at this retreat and was willing to push past these obstacles to get there.

My anxiety had been building over the resignation. I didn't know how we would survive. Larry planned to go into counseling for a living, and I had taken a part-time job as a secretary, using skills from a half-year of typing class I took in ninth grade. I felt restless and had trouble sleeping. I would wake in the middle of the night with my heart pounding. The nerves in my shoulders tingled. *Would we have to sell our home?* There were so many unanswered questions swirling through my mind. The uncertainty of our future consumed me that first weekend of November.

I knew from previous years that the woman's retreat was a good place to relax and be refreshed. Over one hundred women gathered every year in anticipation of creating a special memory. Friendships were forged around dinner tables, laughter filled the hallways, and God's Spirit nourished our souls through the worship and inspirational speakers. I didn't want to miss out, and I felt the tension leave my neck and shoulders soon after I arrived.

Muriel Sandbo was our gifted retreat speaker that year. A stately, beautiful, Norwegian woman with a quiet spirit and deep knowledge of God's Word, she knew how to reach into the hearts of women. We had met previously, but Muriel didn't know me well. She didn't know Larry was resigning. She didn't know we had two teenage sons.

The Friday night meeting began with a typical Pennsylvania Dutch smörgåsbord dinner. Friendly servers passed platters filled with chicken and dumplings, roast turkey, stuffing, cranberry salad, sauerkraut and pork, corn pudding, and mashed potatoes. We ended with an array of baked pies ala mode. After taking a break to allow the room to be rearranged, we sat conference-style, and our godly speaker stood before us.

CHAPTER 5: "I WILL NOT LET YOU FALTER"

Following a time of worship, Muriel asked the women who wanted special prayer to come to the front of the room. Before I could move, she looked straight at me and said, "Annalee, come up here." I was sure she wanted me to come and pray for the women. *Oh, no! I have nothing to give! I'm too exhausted!*

I stood up slowly and walked up to Muriel. I stood beside her, creating a sharp contrast to her appearance with my short stature, and dark hair and olive complexion.

To my great surprise, Muriel took me in her arms!

I began to cry.

"Let go of the fear," she said. "Let go of the guilt."

She continued to hold me as the tears flowed and sobs pulsed through my body. Her words were a catalyst for my surrender. I knew God was speaking to me. My muscles relaxed and my fear left.

"Larry is going to be okay. Your sons are going to be okay."

I quietly listened as she supported my body with her strong arms and continued to speak.

"I have called you from your mother's womb. I will not let you falter. You are graven in my hand."

With these prophetic words, I felt my knees weaken. *Oh, no! Not that!!* I tried to resist, but gently fell to the floor under the power of the Holy Spirit. I was engulfed in light. I couldn't move. I didn't want to move. I felt the incredible peace of my Heavenly Father permeating my whole being. I consciously heard women all over the room begin to cry and gently fall under the power of God's Spirit. Others praised the Lord.

One of my elderly aunts, who attended the retreat, knelt by me and whispered, "Are you okay.?"

I nodded. A couple of hours passed.

Abandoning her prepared teaching, Muriel shared with the women her thoughts on what was happening.

"The Holy Spirit is doing a deep, healing work in many of your lives. Allow Him to do what He desires," she encouraged us.

Later, Muriel helped me stand up. She looked deep into my eyes and said, "I don't know what I was saying. Do you have sons?"

"Yes, two."

She put her hand to her chest and whispered that she felt something flow out of her spirit into me. I agreed that I felt a deep, spiritual exchange between us.

The rest of the weekend is a blur. Early Sunday morning, I lay in the back seat of the car of the two women who offered to take me home. We arrived at the church just in time for me to walk down the aisle and sit on the front row as the service began. During worship we sang, "When I Look into Your Holiness." I raised my hands in praise, and tears streamed down my cheeks as I recalled my experience on Friday night.

My voice joined the congregation, "I worship You, I worship You. The reason I live is to worship You." I had seen the beauty of the Lord on that retreat.

After the time of worship, my husband asked me to come to the platform. Larry announced his resignation, then asked the congregation to sing, "Arise and Sing, Ye Children of Zion." We stood together looking out over the congregation. Some were people I had known all my life. Others we had come to know and love during the past two years of pastoral ministry. I began to cry again.

There would be many, many more tears. I had no idea what was in my future. I only knew that God would be with me.

CHAPTER 5: "I WILL NOT LET YOU FALTER"

* * * * * * * *

INSIGHTS TO GROW BY

"God, who has called you into fellowship with his Son Jesus Christ our Lord, is faithful" (1 Corinthians 1:9).

God doesn't leave us to flounder our way through life like a ship without a sail. Although we may feel alone in our troubles, He has promised to be with us. God can't go against His Word. Our feelings may scream at us that we've been abandoned, but the truth of God's Word still remains. The words of the Psalmist reinforce this reality: "God is our refuge and strength, an ever-present help in trouble" (Psalm 46:1). When we belong to Jesus, God is always present and provides what we need when we need it. Our Heavenly Father is faithful. Even when our faith wavers, He remains faithful.

I had attended the women's retreat with a heavy heart. I could see my life falling apart. Because I'd been called to ministry as a teenager, I had carried a weight of guilt into that conference room with me. I questioned whether I was betraying God's call on my life. I didn't know what path our lives would take, and how we could still remain in ministry if Larry left the pastorate.

I lived in constant fear at the prospect of losing everything in my life that was meaningful, familiar, and comfortable. I feared for my teenage sons as instability enveloped our home life. The changes in my husband compounded my fear and anxiety.

When Muriel took me in her arms and told me to let go of these powerful, negative emotions that had a grip on my heart and mind, I completely relaxed. As she spoke from her heart, I knew her words were from the Lord, speaking directly to me in my distress. God knew I needed to be reassured of His presence with me. I needed to know that my husband and children would be okay. I needed every word that God spoke through Muriel. They would be the bedrock for my life as I walked into the unknown future.

My experiences since that time haven't included such a dramatic encounter with God as that night in 1988. When I'm going through a troubled time, if I listen, God speaks to me through His Word, other Christians, a sermon, a devotion, or a song on the radio. The Lord will give us the words we need to hear so that we can be victorious in every situation. He wants us to succeed and come out of our troubles as stronger, spiritually healthier disciples.

God's Spirit keeps us in our trials. Only by His power can we find our way through the changes in life. It is the Lord "… who is able to keep you from falling and to present you before his glorious presence without fault and with great joy—to the only God our Savior be glory, majesty, power and authority, through Jesus Christ our Lord, before all ages, now and forevermore! Amen" (Jude 24, 25).

God is faithful! He will provide everything you need in every circumstance. Trust Him with your whole life.

****

PRAYER

Lord, thank You for Your love and faithfulness. You are greater than any problem we can face in life. Your faithfulness is to the heavens! Help us to listen for Your voice in the midst of the storm. Give us ears to hear You speaking to us. Reassure us of Your constant presence. And we will give You the glory! In Jesus' name, Amen.

CHAPTER SIX

MY TURN

"Even though I walk through the valley of the shadow of death,
I will fear no evil, for you are with me."
—Psalm 23:4

After the new year, Larry resigned as pastor of the church. He resigned his credentials with our denomination. His attempts to make a living by counseling were failing. We were struggling financially, and I could see our world crashing in around us.

One cold February night, while our sons were at youth group, Larry and I sat in the family room watching TV. He reached over to me and I cuddled next to him, thinking he wanted to bridge the emotional chasm that had grown between us. As I sat there hoping for a response from him, he began to speak words I never thought I would hear.

"I'm thinking of leaving."

"What? Leaving? Why?"

My words seemed to cling to the back of my throat as I tried to force them out into the now chilled air. My lungs couldn't draw air, and I felt suspended in time. I was unable to think clearly.

"I'm thinking of leaving, but I haven't made up my mind yet," Larry continued.

Stunned and afraid, I was incapable of responding with any sense of sanity.

"Well, thank you for not leaving," were the only words I allowed to pass my lips. I thought if I didn't overreact, maybe he would change his mind.

I said "good night" and climbed the stairs to bed. I heard Larry leave the house, and tears streamed down my cheeks as I lay my head on my pillow. Soon, I drifted off to sleep. I wasn't aware of when he came home and got into bed.

The next morning, I could sense something happening in the deep recesses of my mind. I began to feel the pangs of something dark and deep that wanted to come out. I knew it had something to do with my childhood. I called my mother.

"Mom, who lived next door to us as I was growing up?" I asked.

She quickly gave me the names of the family members who lived in the brown-shingled house next to ours. With each name, something quaked inside of me. I knew it was them. I knew it was both father and son.

"Oh, God," I cried out after hanging up. "What was it? What happened? What am I trying to remember?"

My mind felt like a computer that repeats the message "searching...searching" when someone asks for information. *What am I trying to remember? What is it?*

By evening, Larry arrived home and I told him what was happening. We went to bed that night, and at 3:00 a.m. I awoke terrified. The room was pitch black. The silence felt foreboding. I shook Larry awake. He walked me through the memories of the tragedy of rape. The truth was out. We had both been sexually abused. I knew in that instant that I was looking into the face of evil. I felt engulfed in darkness. The long-buried trauma and terror of my childhood was back with full force.

As I lay in bed crying, Larry held me and assured me, "I won't leave as long as you are having these memories and you're working towards healing." The fear of abandonment from his announcement the previous night had brought up the memories that had been buried for 36 years. It was how I survived. *But would I survive the healing? Would our marriage survive the abuse and what it had done to us?*

The next morning as I got ready to leave for work, Larry asked me, "How old are you, Annalee?"

"I'm four years old," I said without a thought. The words shocked me.

I cried all the way to work that day.

With the help of a co-worker, I found a Christian, female counselor who worked with abuse survivors. I began the long and difficult road to healing. Each time I ascended the stairs to Anne's office, my legs felt like cement blocks were strapped to them. I remember our first session.

"So, how long do you think this is going to take?" I inquired. "Three months or so?"

Anne smiled and gently replied, "Let's just take it one session at a time."

After a few sessions, I asked her for her diagnosis. She told me that I had acute anxiety disorder. With her disclosure, I understood so much about myself that had confused me. Now, the feelings of panic or paranoia that would come on me at times had an explanation. Anne validated my feelings in a way I had never experienced before.

I wasn't sure how I was going to pay for counseling, but I knew I needed help. I began to read profusely on the subject of sexual abuse and its aftereffects, and I knew I didn't want to stay in the place where I was. I didn't want my perpetrators to have the rest of my life. I'd already been robbed of 36 years of living a healthy, whole life. They wouldn't get another day!

When I was alone in my house, I would experience flashbacks of the abuse. In a fetal position on my living room floor, I groaned and wept. I grieved as if I'd lost a daughter. But the child I'd lost was *me*. I lost *myself*—the essence of my person-hood. My emotions, mind and psyche were frozen at the age of four. Now I was carrying them around in a forty-year-old body.

Larry became more and more distant in our relationship. We were both in an enormous amount of shock and pain. We were both changing and didn't know how to relate to each other as we emerged out of the ashes of abuse. There were so many unanswered questions. *Why did God allow this to happen? Why was this all coming up now? What would happen to us and our family?*

One day, Larry asked, "Where was God when I was being abused?"

I didn't have an answer to his question.

"I don't know, Larry. But I do know that if sexual abuse is too hard for God, then we have no hope of healing. If it *isn't* too hard for Him, then He is our ONLY hope. I don't know why this is happening. But I do know I want to be well."

"Then we are moving in opposite directions," Larry said angrily. "I don't believe God is there anymore. And I don't believe Jesus is the Son of God."

My thoughts scrambled to understand what he'd just said. I felt grieved by his words, but I avoided any further discussion.

CHAPTER 6: MY TURN

As I searched the Scriptures for stability and sanity, the words of Jeremiah 32:17 spoke to me: "Ah, Sovereign Lord, you have made the heavens and the earth by your great power and outstretched arm. Nothing is too hard for you." The Lord brought assurance that sexual abuse was not beyond His grace. I knew that God knew me better than I could ever know myself, and that He was the One who would bring healing as I surrendered the pain to Him.

I listened to the voice of the Lord through my suffering. He told me that I'd been left with a broken spirit. Anger, fear, and shame had hounded my life in the wake of the abuse. He wanted to heal me and replace the anger with forgiveness, the fear with peace, and the shame with joy. Knowing I was desperate for comfort, the Lord kept reinforcing His promises to me. Psalm 34 says, "The Lord is close to the brokenhearted and saves those who are crushed in spirit" (v.18). Abuse was not beyond God's power to heal.

Each day was a battle with fear. I felt like I was walking on a tree branch in the darkness and didn't know if my next step would be supported by the branch, or if I would fall into an abyss. I had learned how to live my life with the effects of the abuse. I had reacted to life out of the wounds of my childhood. I understood that I needed to mature and respond, rather than react, to life's circumstances. Learning to walk the road to wholeness was scary—it felt so unfamiliar.

Some days, I didn't know if I would survive. Often, the words of Muriel Sandbo came back to me. "I have called you from your mother's womb. I will not let you falter. You are graven in my hand." I found reassurance in knowing that the Lord knew what my future held when I attended that retreat. He knew I would need something to hold on to. And He graciously gave it to me.

A few weeks after the initial memories, I went to choir practice. The director passed out sheet music to practice for the following Sunday. It was titled, "The Majesty and Glory of Your Name," written by Tom Fettke and Linda Lee Johnson and based on Psalm 8, the same chapter I read as a child sitting on my bed. It was no accident. As we rehearsed the music, I sang the words through my tears, "Little children praise You perfectly, and so would we, and so would we." The chorus rang out, "Hallelujah, hallelujah!" The Lord was telling me to keep praising Him as I did in my childhood—trusting Jesus completely. My healing would come as I praised the God who is higher than our circumstances and holds each of us in the palm of His hand.

The next day, I approached my desk at the real estate office. Before settling in to sift through the pile of papers waiting for me, I flipped the page of my daily calendar. It read, "Praise is more spontaneous when things go right; but it is more precious when things go wrong." (Author unknown.)

I sent up a prayer, *Okay, Lord, give me the grace to keep praising You on this journey!*

* * * * * * * *

INSIGHTS TO GROW BY

"But when he, the Spirit of truth comes, he will guide you into all truth" (John 16:13).

Jesus said, "You will know the truth and the truth will set you free" (John 8:32). Jesus spoke of Himself as the truth. John 14:6 says, "Jesus answered, 'I am the way and the truth and the life. No one comes to the Father except through me.'" When we come to Jesus, we learn the truth about who we are and who He is. The Spirit of God reveals the truth about our sin and our need of a Savior. As we receive Jesus into our hearts, we are set free from our sin. The bondage of our sinful nature no longer has its hold on our lives, and we are free to live a life pleasing to God.

Yet, there is another aspect of knowing the truth that is involved in being set free. It is the truth about our woundedness, our brokenness. As long as we are carrying a broken heart, we will be in bondage to the hidden thoughts and damaged emotions it produces. The Holy Spirit wants to reveal the hidden things in our lives that keep us from being free to love and serve God with our whole being.

The day I cried out to the Lord from the winged chair in my living room, I began a long journey of healing. It was the gentle leading of the Spirit that brought me to that place. For several months, the Holy Spirit drew me back to my chair in the living room. I felt Him urging me to come aside and spend time with Him. My devotional life had always been sporadic. Now I felt God's Spirit drawing me, compelling me to seek Him. He knew the journey to wholeness would be painful and difficult. He knew the path would make me vulnerable. He strengthened me for the moment of truth. I felt His cushioning arms under me. Deuteronomy 33:27 says: "The eternal God is your refuge, and underneath are the everlasting arms." God's arms are strong enough to hold us through the most tragic events of our lives. His love is there to hold us in the pain. As I began my journey, I felt cocooned in the warmth of His love.

The Lord knows the perfect time and means to get us to the point where we desire change. He allowed the circumstances of my life to bring me to a point of crisis. It was then that He was able to do the deep work that was needed in order to set me free from the bondage of my painful childhood. Looking back, I can see His hand in the events that brought me to the place where I could remember the abuse and release the memories to Him. I had to make a conscious choice to trust Jesus for my healing.

As the shock wore off, I could look back and see the goodness of the Lord in my childhood. He hadn't allowed the abuse to kill me. I gave my heart to Jesus at a young age. Jesus rescued me from a life that could have been filled with enormous suffering and addiction—a life bent on self-destruction. As I praised Him for His goodness and sovereignty in my life, my heart began the slow but permanent process of healing. Praise was an important key to finding the life I'd longed for—a life free of fear, anger and shame.

* * * * * * *

PRAYER

Lord Jesus, You created us, and You know every fiber of our being. While You walked this earth, You suffered. You know the pain of abuse. As our Great Physician, You can heal both body and soul. Please wrap Your loving arms around our broken and crushed spirits. Please heal the memories of our past and give us hope that only You can give. Deliver us from evil as we lift our hearts in praise to You, our Sovereign Lord. In Jesus' name, Amen

A PAINFUL DEPARTURE

"Never will I leave you, never will I forsake you."
—Hebrews 13:5

We survived Thanksgiving with my extended family at my parents' home, but I knew we were in trouble. The next night, Larry stayed out until 2:00 a.m. When he came in the front door, I was still awake, waiting in the winged chair in our living room. I had spent many, many nights waiting for Larry during our marriage. In the past, I had looked out the window of our home and prayed for his return. He always seemed to have a good reason for staying out later than I had anticipated.

But that night, I was angry. With his threat to leave still fresh in my mind, I found the courage to confront him.

"Where have you been? Why don't you call me when you are staying out so late? What's going on?"

"I'm leaving you after the holidays."

"I thought you said you wouldn't leave until I had gone through the healing process from the abuse."

"I can't stay. I'm not happy with you. And if you were honest, you'd admit you haven't been happy for the past ten years."

"That's not true," I said. My voice escalated in pitch. I felt frustrated and angry. "There have been things I thought we should work on. But I haven't been unhappy all these years."

"I'm telling you now, I'm leaving after Christmas."

"Let's get counseling first." I tried to lower my voice so our sons wouldn't awake with the tone of our conversation. "We have 20 years of a foundation to work from. Don't just toss everything we have."

"I'm leaving. That's final. I'll be gone in January." Then he added, "Do you want me to sleep on the couch tonight?"

Still reeling from his announcement, I took a moment to breathe deeply.

"No," I whispered through the thick, dark clouds that had engulfed my soul. I bowed my head and muttered softly, "It's still your bed."

I slowly climbed the stairs, praying as I would for the next month that somehow he would change his mind; that he wouldn't be able to leave our sons; that God would work a miracle and it wouldn't happen.

During the next few weeks, I pleaded with God for my family. One day, when everyone was out of the house, I went upstairs to my bedroom and closed the door. I knelt down and leaned over far enough for my face to meet the carpet. As I wet the carpet with my tears, my voice rang out in desperation. I wailed like a woman drowning in her grief.

"Please, Jesus. Don't let this happen. Don't let him leave our family. Please, God, intervene. Have mercy. Don't let him leave.

CHAPTER 7: A PAINFUL DEPARTURE

Don't let him leave!"

Exhausted from the emotional workout I had experienced, I crawled to my bed and lay down. As I nodded off to sleep, I gave my breaking heart to God. I knew the future was out of my control—and so was Larry.

Over the days that followed, I tried to prepare for Christmas. I loved to make gifts, bake cookies, and decorate our home for the celebration of our Lord Jesus. The kitchen and adjoined family room were especially fun. Hunter green and red were the primary colors that adorned the space. Tiny white lights on the tree in the corner of the family room seemed to make it look like a Saks Fifth Avenue window display.

One of my usual stops in search of Christmas gifts was the local Christian bookstore. That year, I walked down the aisle toward the music cassettes to see what was new. I noticed a Christmas album by Michael W. Smith. I purchased a couple, one for our family, and one as a gift, and continued with my shopping.

When I arrived home, I carefully removed the plastic wrap and inserted the tape into our cassette player. The music was glorious. Lively, contemporary renditions of familiar and not-so-familiar Christmas music filled our home. One song in particular drew my attention. It started with the solo voice of a young boy singing, "All is well, all is well."

I sat in the family room on the green, cushioned arm chair listening with my ears and my heart. As the words echoed across the room, I felt cushioned in the arms of God. A choir joined the child's voice and together they sang the heavenly words, "All is well, all is well, Lift up your voice and sing!"

With tears streaming down my face, I called out to the Lord, "All is not well. Larry says he's going to leave. All is not well, Jesus. All is not well." I buried my face in my hands and sobbed.

The voice of Jesus responded to my aching heart, "Yes, All IS well, Annalee. Because I came to earth, you have my love and you have hope. All is well, because I am alive." I chose to believe what my heart was hearing. Although in my finite mind, I couldn't begin to imagine how all would be well, I put my trust in Jesus and received His peace in return.

On Christmas Eve I wrapped gifts while sitting on our bed as I had done in previous years. I loved our bedroom. I had carefully chosen delicate mauve colors for the carpet and wallpaper. It was a safe, peaceful place for Larry and me to share our life together.

That year, I lay on my bed and cried. With each gift I wrapped for Larry, the tears flowed. He loved sweaters, and I had chosen a beautiful black and gray cardigan for him. As I went through the motions of wrapping, my fear-filled mind robbed me of the joy of the season. *What was going to happen? Would he really leave? Was this our last Christmas together?* I was in such turmoil. Between my abuse surfacing and Larry threatening to leave, I was drowning emotionally. I honestly didn't believe he could leave.

I don't remember much about the holidays. I went through the celebrations trying to hide my fear and sadness from my family.

Soon after, Larry and I were riding in his car when he looked at me and said, "Did you remember that I said I would leave after the holidays?"

Stiff with fear, my hands neatly folded in my lap, I whispered, "Yes, I remember."

"Don't you think I will leave?" he yelled.

Startled by his outburst, I didn't respond. Now I wasn't only afraid of him leaving, I was afraid of *HIM*. I didn't know who he was anymore. I didn't recognize the person that was emerging. It didn't feel like the man I had known for the past 20 years. I wasn't sure I wanted to be with this person.

CHAPTER 7: A PAINFUL DEPARTURE

The tension between us increased over the next few days. *How could he do this? Why would he do this?* Feeling confused and rejected, I pushed through my daily activities, silently pleading with God for an answer to what was happening between us.

The day before he left, I stood in the shower. As the water cascaded down my body, my tears mingled with the water and were swept away down the drain. I groaned. Bent over in pain I prayed, "Please just take my breath now. I can't live through this. I can't live through him walking out of our marriage. I can't live through him telling our sons he is leaving. I don't want to live anymore."

My prayer wasn't answered. I kept breathing. I wasn't sure why.

The next day, on the first Sunday in January, I went to church with my sons as usual. During the service, I prayed silently, *God, don't let him do this. Don't let him leave.* I looked around at the congregation. Not a soul knew what I hid in my heart. I hadn't told anyone about Larry's threat to leave. I thought if I didn't speak the words, maybe it wouldn't happen.

When I got home after church, I pulled up to the house to see Larry's car packed with clothes and boxes of personal belongings. My heart sank. I was nauseated and felt light-headed. As I pulled into the driveway, I prayed for protection and wisdom. The Lord spoke clearly to me. "Be still and know that I am God" (Psalm 46:10).

"But, Lord, he's leaving. Everything is falling apart."

"Be still." I heard the words once again.

I gathered my courage and went into the house. My sons had gone out with their church friends for lunch, and it was just the two of us.

I lay on the couch in the family room and cried. Larry came in and sat down at the kitchen table. Soon, he cried, too. We stayed silent and wept. He finally broke the silence.

"I don't want to leave this house," he said.

I noticed he didn't say he didn't want to leave *me*.

"Why are you doing this?" I asked. "Why are you throwing everything away?"

Larry didn't respond.

Our oldest son, Larry Jr., came through the front door. He went upstairs, and I followed him. Larry came into our son's room shortly after and found us sitting on the bed.

"Why is your car packed with your clothes, Dad?" Larry Jr. asked angrily of his father.

"I'm leaving your mother. I'm not happy anymore."

"Leaving?" my son yelled. He stood up and addressed his father.

"What do you mean you are leaving? What about God's love? You preached that we could draw on God's love when we run out of human love!"

"That doesn't work for me anymore," his father answered.

My eighteen-year-old son started to cry. His face wrenched with pain, he looked at me and said, "I thought you said this would never happen!"

Feeling his pain, I sobbed, "I never thought it would."

"I'm leaving tonight," Larry told him. "I want to see if I want a divorce. I'll give it a few months and let you know what I decide."

My son ran into the bathroom. I followed closely behind.

"You told me this wouldn't happen—that you and Dad would never divorce each other."

"I'm sorry, Larry," I sobbed. "I don't want a divorce. I never thought this would happen to us."

"What are you going to do?"

"I don't know. I can't stop him from leaving. I don't know what to do."

My son was on Christmas break from his freshman year in college. After he wiped his tears, he descended the stairs. He picked up his packed suitcase that he'd placed by the front door in anticipation of his ride back to school. He said nothing more to his father. I went to the door with him, reached up to his six-foot-two-inch stature, and held him. I tried to impart courage and comfort to him.

"We're going to be okay," I said. "We're going to be okay."

Larry left the house shortly after our son and said he would return later to tell our younger son, Ryan, that he was leaving. I felt angry that he was putting us all through such an excruciating experience. A few minutes after Larry left the house, Ryan returned from lunch with his friends. I remained silent about what his brother and I had just experienced.

Ryan and I went to the evening service at our church. I sat in the balcony, hoping that no one could see the pain in my eyes from my bleeding heart. At the conclusion of the service, my friend Eloise came over to me. The tears flowed, and I blurted out to her, "Larry is preparing to leave me. He told Larry Jr. today that he is leaving so he can decide if he wants a divorce."

"Oh, no," she said as she put her arms around me in her loving way. "I'm so sorry. Let me pray with you."

She prayed for a few minutes. Years later, Eloise told me that she and her husband cried through the night when they heard that Larry had left. They had been dear friends. As young women, Eloise and I had become pregnant around the same time. We reared our sons together in the church. We shared many happy times and carried many wonderful memories in our hearts.

Eloise and I hugged after she prayed. Then Ryan and I left for home. Larry returned to our house to tell Ryan he was leaving. My son remained quiet and listened to his father's announcement. His face became ashen and tears filled his eyes. I hugged him and he made his way up the stairs to bed.

A short time after Larry left the house, the phone rang.

"I can't find the key to the place where I was going to stay tonight," he said sheepishly. "Can I sleep on the couch in the family room just for one night?"

"No! You can't."

"But I have nowhere to sleep."

"Find a place!"

I was in so much pain, I couldn't believe what I had just heard. *He just tore our family apart and now he wants to come back in the house and sleep on the couch!*

I had set the first boundary between us. I was tired of Larry controlling my life through fear and bringing such pain and turmoil into the lives of our sons. I crawled into bed and turned off the light. My pillow soaked with tears, I drifted off to sleep, only to wake and cry several times through the night. The bed felt cold without Larry. I felt so alone.

I cried to the Lord and begged Him to comfort me. His presence filled my heart, and He reminded me that He would never leave me or forsake me.

I whispered, *Thank You, Lord, thank You. But I want both You AND Larry in my life. Why is this happening? Why, why?*

The next morning, I called my mother to tell her Larry had

gone. She broke down and cried as I told her what had happened. I don't remember her prayers, but she lifted me to the Lord over the phone. It was a comfort to know that my mother was always there for me and willing to share in my pain. When our conversation ended, she offered to come to my house so I wouldn't feel alone. Of course, I agreed.

My next phone call was to Anne, my counselor.

"He really left. I didn't think he would do it, but he left," I cried to the woman I had learned to trust with my deepest feelings.

"I'm so sorry. What did you say to him as he was leaving?" she asked.

"I asked him why he was doing this, but he didn't reply. I didn't try to stop him. I didn't say anything."

"That's all?"

I heard her sigh in frustration. She had been trying to get me to confront Larry about his threat to leave over the past few weeks. I hadn't had the courage to do it.

I told her, "The Lord told me to be still and know that he is God" (Psalm 46:10).

A deluge of emotion poured out. I barely got the words out through my sobs. "Why has God left me? Where is He? Why is He letting this happen? I prayed. I fasted. I pleaded. But He let it happen anyway. I don't understand. What did I do wrong?"

Anne listened while I poured out my pain. Then she spoke words I will never forget.

"Take your hand out of Larry's hand and put it in the hand of God. You're not alone. The darkness is the shadow of God."

Her words calmed me enough for me to catch my breath. Slowly, my tears subsided. My anger retreated for a moment.

"Thank you, Anne. I needed to hear that. I feel so alone right now."

"You're not alone. God is with you. He's closer now than he has ever been before."

"It doesn't feel that way, but I'll trust what you are telling me."

I confirmed a counseling appointment for the following week and hung up the phone. After another deep breath, I gathered my courage and went upstairs into Ryan's room. Still sleepy, he got out of bed and walked across the hall, over to the window of his brother's room. He looked out toward the street where his father always parked his car. Turning to me with quivering lips and tear-filled eyes, he asked, "Is he really gone?"

"Yes. He's really gone."

We put our arms around each other and cried. My heart was heavy with sadness for my fifteen-year-old son.

"I'm sorry. I couldn't stop him. I'm sorry," I said as we dried our tears.

Within twenty minutes my mother was at the front door, and as she walked into our home, we hugged and cried. Then she hugged Ryan. I gave him permission to stay home from school, and my mother and I did what we usually did when we were stressed. We cleaned the house! The energy from our anger and confusion went into forceful cleaning that made the rooms sparkle.

By that afternoon, my son Larry was on the phone.

"I'm coming home. I'm afraid Dad will do something to hurt you and Ryan," he said.

"No," I assured him. "Your father has never been violent with me. I'm okay. You stay in college. Your brother and I will be fine."

"I cried in the shower," his voice cracked as he spoke. "I cried until I couldn't cry any more. But I've promised myself I won't cry over this again."

"It's good to cry, Larry. This is painful. Tell Jesus how you feel and let Him heal your heart."

After assuring him once again that Ryan and I were okay, I hung up the phone only to have it ring. It was Eloise.

"A group of women want to meet with you and pray," she said. "Can you come to the church one day this week for prayer?"

"Yes, sure." I said, feeling grateful. "I can come on Tuesday. Let me know if that is good for the other women. Thank you. Thank you, dear friend."

I already felt less alone. The reassurances of my family and friends brought comfort. These loving people were going to help me on this journey. They were a visible source of God's presence. The journey would be a long, hard one, and I needed all the support they could give.

****

INSIGHTS TO GROW BY

"Because you are my help, I sing in the shadow of your wings" (Psalm 63:7).

When we face trouble and trials in our lives, we sense darkness closing in on us. The light is dim in the cavern of our souls, and we may feel abandoned by God. We can't sense His presence, and our days are filled with clouds that hover over our minds, refusing to allow any light to penetrate our fears and anxieties about the future.

Most of us have learned to fear shadows. Shadows typically mean a storm is brewing, the night is falling, or someone or something is lurking around a corner. But when we belong to Jesus, when we are covered with the blood that was shed for us on Calvary's cross, we don't need to fear the shadows. According to Psalm 63, the darkness is not the absence of the presence of the Lord, but the shadow of His wings. Our loving Lord hovers over us like a mother hen covering her chicks from danger. The darkness may feel frightening at first, but God has actually moved closer to us, bending over us during our time of trouble, ready and willing to help us as we lean on Him—safe under the shadow of His wings. The Lord can help us reinterpret the darkness to see that He has been with us all along.

Romans chapter 8 tells us that nothing, absolutely nothing can separate us from the love of God. When we have trusted Jesus for our salvation, nothing and no one on earth can sever us from His unfailing love. Our emotions scream that we have been abandoned when we are in pain, but God's Word tells us that is impossible. And God keeps His Word. He'll never forsake those that belong to Him.

As I was growing up in "old Ebenezer" church, one of my favorite hymns spoke about being sheltered under the wings of God. As the Psalmist wrote, it is possible to sing in the shadow of His wings. I still sing the words of William O. Cushing more than fifty years later:

UNDER HIS WINGS
(LYRICS BY WILLIAM O. CUSHING; MUSIC BY IRA D. SANKEY)

Under His wings I am safely abiding,
Tho' the night deepens and tempests are wild,
Still I can trust Him;
I know He will keep me.
He has redeemed me, and I am His child.
Under His wings, under His wings,

Who from His love can sever?
Under His wings my soul shall abide,
Safely abide forever.

The third verse is as beautiful as the first:

Under His wings—O what precious enjoyment!
There will I hide till life's trials are o'er;
Sheltered, protected, no evil can harm me.
Resting in Jesus, I'm safe evermore.

When Larry left, I thought God had left me, too. But the truth is that God was right there with me. I was sheltered and protected by the Creator of the universe, the true Lover of my soul.

Have you ever felt abandoned? It doesn't matter if it was a spouse, a parent, or a friend. The pain is overwhelming. It tears at our hearts and leaves us devastated. We feel rejected and worthless. Remember that God values you and will never abandon you. Allow Him to shelter you with His wings and love you back to a place of wholeness.

****

PRAYER

Lord, we thank You for Your promise never to leave or forsake us. When our hearts are breaking, help us to remember that You are sheltering us under Your wings. Remind us that as we lean on You in the darkness, You will bring us once again to a place of light. Give us a song to sing as we wait for Your help. In Jesus' name, Amen.

CHAPTER EIGHT

A BROKEN HEART

"Blessed are those who mourn, for they will be comforted."
—Matthew 5:4

The reality of my life came rushing in like whitewater rapids, carrying me downstream, bouncing me around, and threatening to swallow me whole. Any illusion of control was gone. My denial of "this can't be happening to me" was quickly replaced by the impact of what I faced. Larry was gone.

I appreciated the prayers that were said on my behalf. I met with my friends at the church a couple of times and felt peaceful after our times of intercession. But when I returned home, I was faced with my loneliness and anxiety.

I had no way of supporting myself and my sons. My salary at the real estate office paid for food and minimal household expenses. The mortgage payments had stopped. At first, Larry offered to pay the utility bills and gave me money to help support Ryan. Then one day, I came home from work and my electricity and gas were shut off. When I called the utility companies, they told me I owed hundreds of dollars. Larry had stopped paying the bills and failed to inform me. I was furious. *How could he just stop paying the utilities and not tell me?*

My church came to the rescue. After I called the minister of pastoral care and explained the situation, a check was issued from the benevolence fund so my utilities could be reinstated.

The incident forced me to recognize that Larry was not coming back, and he couldn't be depended upon to take care of us any longer.

I was terrified. When I married Larry, I had never been self-supporting. I'd never been "on my own." To be faced with the sudden responsibility of supporting myself and my sons was paralyzing. There were days when I didn't want to get out of bed. I felt myself spiraling downward into depression. I would force my legs off the mattress, hang them over the side of the bed, and struggle to lift my body with my arms to a sitting position. Some days, I fell back into bed and buried my sobs in my pillow.

The questions nagged me. *How can Larry just walk out like this? What did I do wrong? Maybe if I'd been a better Christian wife, he wouldn't have left. What am I going to do? How am I going to live?*

The unanswered questions consumed my thinking. But the emotional devastation took most of my energy. There was so much to grieve. I had lost my childhood to abuse. I felt robbed of my innocence and dignity. I had lost my husband—the man I was supposed to grow old with—the father of my children. I had lost my position in ministry as the wife of a pastor. I had lost my identity as a partner in life and ministry. The losses kept piling up, and I didn't know if I could bear them. The weight was dragging me into an abyss of hopelessness.

My loneliness was exacerbated by the cold, short days. January's desolation reminded me of the emptiness in my heart. Everywhere I went, I felt the sting of my separation. As Valentine's Day approached, I had to face the racks of cards in the local gift store addressed to "My Husband" or "My Sweetheart." I shifted my eyes to the floor as I walked down the aisles. Whenever I saw something that reminded me that I was in a broken marriage, my heart ached.

CHAPTER 8: A BROKEN HEART

It was painful to see other couples walking down the street, holding hands. I felt jealous.

There were days when I cried all the way to work. I carried extra make-up with me to replenish what I had cried off on my route to the office. Sometimes during the work day, I retreated into the restroom to grieve. I'd put more make-up under my swollen eyes and walk back into the office, hoping no one would notice. I'd cry all the way home.

Some days, I wasn't sure what I was grieving. Was I crying for myself? For my children? For my childhood? For Larry? For my marriage? For my shattered dreams? For all the people whose lives were affected by our tragedy? I grieved for it all. The tears flowed; my sleep was tumultuous; my appetite gone. It seemed my life was scattered in pieces on the floor.

More questions came. Why did I marry Larry? Was it God's will for me to marry him, only to have him walk out twenty years later? Why did God let me marry him if he knew Larry would do this?

I pleaded with the Lord, "Please, God, let me know. Was I supposed to marry Larry? Why did You let me marry a man who would abandon me? I always prayed for Your will. Please give me some answers."

Many nights I lay in bed asking, praying, pleading. But no answers came. It seemed like there was a brick wall between God and me. Why was he silent? Didn't he see me in my distress?

Every morning I went to my winged chair, which I named my "prayer chair." I dropped to my knees and poured out my grief to God. I prayed Scripture over my sons, asking God to make them stronger through their pain. I kept asking, knocking and seeking. I was sure that God would hear my persistent cries and do something miraculous. But no miracle came. No one came to my rescue. The church leaders were silent. The district leaders of my denomination didn't call. No one showed up at my front door with a check to pay my mortgage. Larry didn't walk back through the front door of our home.

Then one night while my sons were out of the house, I went upstairs to my bedroom and looked out the window. I raised my fisted arm to God and shouted, "Is this how You treat people who follow Your call into ministry? Is this how You treat Your friends? You'd better show me who You are, because I don't like what I see! Who are You, God? I feel crushed. This is too hard. Have mercy on me." I fell to the floor in a flood of tears with my face in the carpet. Sobs echoed through the room.

My chest physically ached. It seemed there was a large hole in my heart that couldn't be filled. My heart was broken. Exhausted, I crawled into bed. There on my bed, the Lord comforted me. I sensed His presence and drifted off to sleep.

****

INSIGHTS TO GROW BY

"He heals the brokenhearted and binds up their wounds" (Psalm 147:3).

When our hearts are broken, we feel alone and abandoned by God. It's hard to sense His presence when our emotions scream at us and we feel overwhelmed by our circumstances.

There will be times when each of us will question, "Where is God?" Psalm 34 gives us the answer. God is close by. The Lord is very close to those who are suffering from a broken heart or a crushed spirit. Whatever we may feel, the truth that God is with us serves as an anchor for our souls.

In his book *Broken in the Right Place: How God Tames the Soul*, Alan Nelson writes, "The purpose behind brokenness is to remind us that God is sovereign and that we are not." When we are broken, we have to make a choice. Our way, or God's way. We can turn our backs on Him, or surrender everything to Him. We can try to put the pieces together ourselves, or give Him the shattered areas of our lives for Him to put together as He sees fit. We can attempt to "be God" by trying to control our circumstances, or we can recognize His sovereignty and allow Him full dominion.

The benefit of surrendering is that God, our Creator, can make something beautiful from our brokenness. Only He knows the broken places. Only He can heal us and make us better than we were before.

The words of author Roberta Hestenes apply here: "Brokenness is a yielded heart open before God, a heart emptied of pride and self claims, of all arrogance, knowing our sin, our self-deception, our frailty, weakness and inadequacy... Brokenness is not the opposite of wholeness; it is the continuing precondition for it." (Roberta Hestenes, "Personal Renewal: Reflections on 'Brokenness," TSF Bulletin, Nov.-Dec. 1984, p.24)

As we yield our hurts to God, surrender our hopes and dreams to His sovereignty, and ask Him to heal our brokenness, it opens the way for Him to make us whole. As long as we cling to our own ideas of "how life should be," we hinder the work of God in our lives. We will stay stuck in our grief and brokenness. It isn't until we work through our grief and relinquish our illusion of control that we can move into the goodness that God has prepared for us.

While we move towards surrender and trust, the Lord doesn't leave us without comfort. As we mourn our losses, the Holy Spirit brings solace and peace to our souls. When we allow ourselves to feel the sting of our losses, God sends the Holy Spirit, wraps us in His love, and heals our broken hearts.

****

PRAYER

Lord Jesus, You are the healer of broken hearts. Right now, my heart is aching. I feel like I can't bear the pain of my loss any longer. I surrender to Your sovereign will in my life. I let go of all my preconceived ideas of how my life should look and bow at Your throne of grace. Please send Your Holy Spirit to comfort me in my grief. Wrap Your loving arms around me, and give me the peace that passes understanding. In Jesus' name I pray, Amen.

CHAPTER NINE

NEW BEGINNINGS

*"For your Maker is your Husband—the Lord Almighty is his
name—the Holy One of Israel is your Redeemer; he is called the
God of all the earth."*
—Isaiah 54:5

I tried to recover from the memories of abuse and the abandonment by my husband, but my emotions continued to fluctuate on a daily basis. It took but a single thought about my circumstances and my mood plummeted. I tried to keep a positive attitude, but the bright light of hope grew dimmer as I faced each new day. Nothing of my life made sense. I felt hopeless most of the time.

One day while on lunch break, I went to a local bookstore where I found a book that intrigued me. I thought it might help stabilize my emotions. It was *The Spirit of the Disciplines: Understanding How God Changes Lives* by Dallas Willard. In it, he describes disciplines in which Christians need to engage for a victorious life. He writes about Disciplines of Abstinence (solitude, silence, fasting, frugality, chastity, secrecy, sacrifice) and Disciplines of Engagement (study, worship, celebration, service, prayer, fellowship, confession, submission). (HarperSanFrancisco, 1988, p. 158) Determined to incorporate them into my daily living, I awoke each morning at 6:30 a.m.

for prayer and devotions. In the evening, I spent 30 minutes or more reading the Bible. My thoughts and feelings were recorded in journals. I memorized Scripture verses that gave me hope. I set aside one day a week for prayer and fasting. I continued to worship and praise the Lord, even if it was through my tears.

At times, my feelings swung between a sense of peace and expectation of God's intervention, and fear and depression. I felt vulnerable without a husband—with no one to provide for or protect me. There was something more I needed to anchor my soul in this storm.

One night, as I read in the book of Isaiah, I came across a passage in chapter 54 that I had never noticed before. It was as if the words were written just for me. I cried as I had the revelation that God knew exactly what had happened to me. He knew my grief and the shame I felt from the abandonment.

"Do not be afraid; you will not suffer shame.

Do not fear disgrace; you will not be humiliated.

You will forget the shame of your youth and remember no more the reproach of your widowhood.

For your Maker is your husband—the Lord Almighty is his name—the Holy One of Israel is your Redeemer;

He is called the God of all the earth.

The Lord will call you back as if you were a wife deserted and distressed in spirit—

A wife who married young, only to be rejected, says your God" (Isaiah 54: 4-6).

"A wife who married young, only to be rejected." There it was, as clear as crystal! God was not oblivious to my circumstances, but He knew my heartache and would be a husband to me. He would be my

Provider, Protector and Defender. I would lack nothing because His perfect love would sustain me.

It wasn't long before the Lord showed His power to provide. When Larry left, we'd been leasing a Ford Taurus station wagon. A few months after he was gone, the lease expired, and I needed to turn the car back in to the dealership. I didn't have the money to purchase another vehicle. While married, I left the car decisions up to Larry. Now that he was gone, I needed to do something about transportation.

I knew of someone in my church who owned a car dealership, so I called him and told him of my circumstances.

"I just turned my leased car in and need something for transportation. But I don't have much money," I said.

"What are you looking for?" he asked.

"Anything that will run," I said, hoping he couldn't hear the panic in my voice.

"I have an old Chrysler Aries station wagon you are welcome to use. I'll warn you though. It's on its last leg."

I wasn't sure what that meant, but I picked up the car and used it for a couple of months. Then one day, as I was driving to work, I pressed on the brake only to have it go all the way to the floor. The master cylinder had gone. I was terrified, but I had the presence of mind to pull on the emergency brake and slowly steer the car to the side of the road. I had it towed to the parking lot of my church. Then I called the dealer. He said there wasn't much he could do for me.

I don't remember how I got to work, but after a couple of weeks I received a call from a friend who also went to my church. He said he had a surprise for me.

"What is it?" I asked.

"The congregation collected a love offering for you. They gave over $4,000.00, and we've purchased a used car for you. It's a Chevy Celebrity and has low mileage. You can pick it up at the car dealership where you got the Aries."

"Hallelujah!" I praised through my tears. "Thank you, thank you!" I felt love and gratitude well up in my heart for the Body of Christ. This could have been an opportunity for judgment and rejection towards me. Instead, the church extended love, compassion, and generosity to me and my sons. They reflected Jesus' character and helped supply what I needed.

I sent up an additional "thank You" to God and soon felt His presence. Peace entered my soul, and I sensed Him assuring me that He would provide all my needs.

The Lord also showed me the power of His protection on my life. I was convinced that He had rescued me as a child from all the abuse I'd sustained. He didn't allow it to destroy me. But now I was faced with the realization that Larry may have exposed me to the AIDS/HIV virus or other diseases. Fear gripped my soul, but I knew I had to know the truth.

One night the phone rang. It was Larry.

"How are you doing?" he asked.

"What do you care? I'm going to the doctor to be tested for AIDS," I snapped back.

"You don't have to worry about that," he said.

"And why should I trust anything you say?"

That ended our conversation. I phoned a local clinic to schedule AIDS testing. Alone, I climbed the dark stairway to a large, dimly lit room filled with people, mostly students from a local college. As I sat in a chair, waiting for my name to be called, a police officer entered with a young man who was handcuffed and ankle-chained. Startled, I had the urge to run out of the room. *How did I get into this situation? What am I doing here?* I wanted to bolt, but I waited.

After taking the test, my fear kept me from finding out the results. Finally, after three months, I asked my sister to come with me to the clinic for moral support.

The attending nurse took me into an office where I sat down. She told me the results of the test were negative. I gave a deep sigh of relief and stood up to leave the room.

"Wait," the nurse said as she motioned for me to sit back in the chair. "You need to take the test again because of the possibility of getting something from recent sexual activity."

"Don't worry about that!" I assured her. "There hasn't been any."

She looked at me with a surprised look. I thanked her and left as quickly as I could without seeming rude. I was grateful that I'd been protected once again.

The future was still uncertain, but I knew I wasn't alone. God was my new husband. My hope was renewed. I knew he would provide for and protect me.

* * * * * * * *

INSIGHTS TO GROW BY

"Why are you downcast, O my soul? Why so disturbed within me? Put your hope in God, for I will yet praise him, my Savior and my God" (Psalm 42:5).

We all need security in life. We need to know that we are safe and protected from danger and want. Women are especially vulnerable. We are most often the homemakers and child care-givers, so our earning capacity is diminished. Women are still underpaid for the same work that men perform. We are physically more vulnerable and susceptible to crimes of violence. Whether we are married or single, we all need to know that we have someone who cares for us and is watching over us for our peace of mind and emotional health.

The Lord promises that He will be the kind of husband we need. He's the kind of husband that will always provide for us. He'll never run out of resources and will never abandon us. Philippians 4:19 says, "And my God will meet all your needs according to his glorious riches in Christ Jesus." This is one of my favorite Bible verses. God promises to meet all of our needs. Not only some of them, but all of them. Everything we will ever need to live and survive and thrive in life will be available to us, because God knows our needs and is able to provide for us. God has a purpose for our lives, and He is willing and able to provide everything we need to accomplish His will and see His purpose realized.

God uses many sources to provide for us. He uses the church of Jesus Christ. He uses individuals. He uses institutions. And often, He uses someone or something we didn't consider in our time of need. It's important to keep our eyes on the Lord as our source of hope when we're in desperate situations. When we look to Jesus, He'll arrange the circumstances so our needs are met. If we look to others, hoping they'll see how distressed we are, we'll be disappointed and resentful if they don't come to our rescue. Lean on God and His promises in times of need and see how graciously He provides. Then praise Him for His faithfulness.

God also promises to protect us from anything that will thwart His purpose for us. As a husband is expected to protect his wife from things that would harm her physically, emotionally, and spiritually, God hovers over us with a watchful eye to make sure we are sheltered from anything that will destroy us or interfere with our relationship with Him.

CHAPTER 9: NEW BEGINNINGS

Before Jesus was crucified, He prayed for His disciples. The seventeenth chapter of the Gospel of John records Jesus' prayer. In verses 11 and 15 he says, "I will remain in the world no longer, but they are still in the world, and I am coming to you. Holy Father, protect them by the power of your name ---the name you gave me---so that they may be one as we are one. My prayer is not that you take them out of the world but that you protect them from the evil one." Paul reiterates this truth in his second letter to the Thessalonians. He writes in chapter three, verse three, "But the Lord is faithful, and he will strengthen and protect you from the evil one."

Jesus continues to intercede for us before the throne of God. He isn't going to allow anything to overtake us, to destroy us, to snatch us from His hand. He is our protector and will bring us safely to our home in heaven. We can place our hope and trust in Him. He is a faithful husband.

****

PRAYER

Father God, how we love You! Your Word says You, our Maker, are our husband. Whether we are male or female, single or married, You are the One who will provide for us and protect us. You know the needs in our lives, and we bring them to You now. Please, by the power of Your name, meet all our needs according to Your will and for Your glory. Keep us from the evil one and bring us safely home to be with You for all eternity when our time on earth is through. In Jesus' name we pray, Amen.

FACING THE DEMONS

*"In your anger do not sin: Do not let the sun go down while
you are still angry, and do not give the devil a foothold."*
—*Ephesians 4:26, 27*

Arriving home from work one day in early spring, I turned into my housing development to see Larry's car parked in front of the house. My arms went limp on the steering wheel and I sighed. I felt frightened. My hands were shaking by the time I took the key out of the ignition. I slowly walked up to the front door. I paused for a moment while questions darted through my mind. *What is he doing in the house? What does he want? Is it safe to go in?* I never thought Larry was capable of doing what he had done. I wondered what else he was capable of doing. His unexpected visit made me uneasy.

As I opened the door, I could see into the kitchen. There was Larry, fork raised, eating meatballs out of the refrigerator.

"What are you doing?" I asked.

"I came to get some clothes for the warm weather. I hope you don't mind me eating a couple of meatballs," he added.

"Please take all your clothes with you."

Yes, I did mind him eating my meatballs. He'd always bragged about them to his family and friends. But more importantly, I wanted my privacy back. I wanted him to leave. I realized I couldn't allow him to hold on to the key to the house any longer. He hadn't surrendered it to me yet.

Larry left that day, but he and Raymond returned a few weeks later. It was Saturday, and my sons were out of the house. I happened to look out the picture window in the living room when they pulled up and parked in the driveway. Larry got out of his car, and I met him at the entrance to the garage. Raymond followed and leaned against my car. I wasn't aware of their relationship yet, but I knew that Larry was living in Raymond's house, and I felt uncomfortable with this unannounced visit. They smiled and said "hello" as if I should be happy to see them.

By then, the shock of Larry leaving and my fear of him had worn thin, and I was ready to set boundaries for my peace of mind and sense of safety in my home.

"What do you want?" I asked.

"I came to get my tools," he said.

"I would have appreciated a call first. Take your tools."

I went inside the house, and after a few minutes, returned to the garage. It was my opportunity to ask for the keys to the house.

"I want the keys to our house and my mother's house, also," I said.

Larry tried to intimidate me.

"What have you been doing? Have you been inside trying to get the courage to ask me for the keys? Did your counselor help you get the guts to ask me for the keys?" he sneered.

CHAPTER 10: FACING THE DEMONS

His arrogant remarks only stirred my anger. His sarcasm added to my resolve.

"Give me the keys, Larry." I stretched out my hand, palm up.

"Okay. Here's the house key and the one to your mother's house. I don't want them anymore."

He handed them to me, and I told him and Raymond to finish taking the tools and leave. Larry's eyes opened wide as if he was surprised at my boldness. After he and Raymond gave each other a quick glance, they left.

I exhaled and had a feeling of relief and renewed strength. Through my counseling I'd learned what it meant to set boundaries with people, especially those with whom I didn't feel safe. I had learned that it was okay to say "no" to people, something I'd always struggled with. The fear that if I set boundaries I'd push Larry away dissipated that afternoon. With each tiny step towards independence, I became stronger.

But there were demons yet to conquer. After finding out that Larry and Raymond were in a gay relationship, my devastation gave way to anger. The anger grew into rage. I knew that I needed to release it to survive. I made sure that I was journaling and exercising every day, so I could express my anger in healthy ways.

Yet, it kept growing. Anger consumed my thoughts. I wanted revenge. I wanted to retaliate. I needed vindication. Anger locked arms with hatred and grew like an abscess on my heart.

As I sat at my desk at work, real estate agents hurried around me to meet clients and show houses as I daydreamed of ramming my car into the front steps of the house where my husband and his lover lived. I couldn't shake the feeling that there must be something I could do to show how angry I was. For a couple of months, I fought the urge to call Larry and scream at him. Resentment had clung to me like a leech.

It was around 3:00 a.m. that I awoke one night, shaking in the darkness. Beads of perspiration quickly formed on my forehead, and my heart raced as I sat up in bed. I took short, forced breaths and braced myself, palms down on the mattress. It took a moment for my mind to be clear enough to recall the dream I'd just had. I shuddered as the images replayed in my consciousness.

In my dream, I'd walked through our home looking through every room. I peered around door jambs, walked into the bedrooms, and walked up and down the stairs repeatedly. Slowly, I made my way around, trying to find Larry. I was frustrated because I couldn't find him. Where was he hiding? Why couldn't I find him?

As I remembered the dream, my heart raced faster. Scenes from the dream flashed before me, and I winced as I saw myself holding the handle of a large silver knife. I was hunting Larry to kill him. My anger had grown to the point of wanting to kill the man who had deserted me and my children and had hurt us so deeply. The dream frightened me enough to call Anne the next morning and make a counseling appointment.

"I'm capable of murder!" I cried, as I sat in the armchair in her office and shared the dream with her.

"You're capable of dreaming about murder," she replied.

"But I wanted to kill him," I said, "and I don't know what to do with what I'm feeling."

"What are you feeling?"

I hesitated and stuttered as I tried to speak.

"I h-hate him." I paused at the sound of my voice uttering those words. They sent chills down my spine.

"But I'm a Christian. I'm not supposed to hate."

In her usual calm, unruffled, and reassuring tone, she said, "Don't you think God knows how you feel, Annalee? Confess it to Him and ask for help so you can come to forgiveness."

"I don't know how to get to forgiveness," I said. "But I don't want hatred in my heart either."

"Are you willing to forgive?" Anne asked.

"I don't know. Not yet."

"Let me ask you this, Annalee. Are you willing to be willing to forgive?"

I put my head down and thought for a moment. I guess I can handle that much.

"Yes, I'm willing to be willing."

"Then give your anger to God," she said.

"How do I give up the anger I feel? I have a right to be angry."

"Yes," Anne said. "You have a right to be angry, but do you want the consequences of allowing it to consume you? Perhaps if you give up the anger, there'll be nothing left of the relationship. Could that be why you're holding on to it?"

Tears flowed and I reached for a tissue on the end table next to my chair. I looked up at her and knew she'd touched on something deep in my heart. I wasn't willing to give up the anger, because it was all I had left of the marriage relationship. If I let go of the anger and resentment, there would be nothing left. And I needed something, even if it was a life-controlling negative emotion, to keep me connected to Larry. I had spent twenty years being one with him. Part of my identity was being his wife. Who would I be if he were no longer in my life?

I went home and lay face down on the living room floor. I poured my heart out to God. Confessing my hatred and anger, I asked the Lord to remove it from my heart and help me to forgive.

"I need Your grace to forgive, Lord. I can't do this on my own. It's impossible without Your divine help!"

I sobbed, I groaned. I felt like I was wrestling with an unseen demon. The muscles in my arms and legs ached like I'd been running uphill while carrying a cinder block.

I waited for a few minutes before getting up. I anticipated a "feeling" to follow my decision to forgive. It didn't come. As I continued to repeat that mind and heart commitment to forgive, the anger and bitterness diminished.

It took a few months, but eventually, the feeling of forgiveness came. I was free from the burden of anger that had felt like a rock tied around my neck for so long. I accepted the reality that there was no longer anything to connect me with Larry. And it was okay.

God Himself filled the void in my spirit, the gaping hole, left by the abandonment and betrayal. The healing had begun, and I felt the stirrings of gratitude.

*** *** **

INSIGHTS TO GROW BY

"For God is greater than our hearts, and he knows everything" (1 John 3:20).

God is bigger than every negative emotion that we can carry in our hearts—anger, resentment, bitterness, fear, anxiety, worry. His love for us is greater than our hearts, and He is able to handle whatever we're experiencing. He's even big enough to handle our anger at Him. He knows what we are feeling, and He is able to give us the courage and strength to overcome the pain we sense in the deepest places of our being.

Most of us don't see anger as a good emotion. We feel guilty for our anger and try to avoid it or hide it from others, acting like "everything is fine!" But God has given us anger as a way of letting us know that something is wrong. Anger can serve to protect us, help us overcome evil with good, help us fight for justice, and propel us to be an advocate for those without a voice. We get into trouble when we act on our anger in ways that hurt ourselves and others or allow it to grow into hatred.

I learned from my experience with hatred that we are all capable of evil. Growing up as a Christian I remember thinking, at the report of a horrible act that someone had committed, "Oh, I'd never do that!" What I couldn't understand as a child is that there is a dark side to our hearts. When we allow anger to fester, it grows into bitterness, and Satan gets a foothold in that weak place. If we allow it to be unchecked and ignore the voice of the Holy Spirit who seeks to help us, we can be as evil as those we see in the world who don't have a relationship with God. We are all capable of unspeakable things without Jesus in our lives. None of us is exempt from committing acts of hatred.

But there is hope. God's grace is available to everyone who cries out to Him. We can't have victory over our circumstances without God's grace—His unmerited favor. It is by His power that we can live above the pain and suffering inflicted by those around us—people we trusted who have wounded us, even evil acts of strangers. His grace is available in every situation. 2 Corinthians 12: 9 reads, "My grace is sufficient for you, for my power is made perfect in weakness." When we are weak, He is our strength! He enables us to do what we are incapable of doing in our human frailty.

Forgiveness is not an option for a follower of Jesus Christ. If we fail to forgive, it affects our relationship with God and interferes with our spiritual growth. When Jesus shared His example of how to pray with His disciples, known as the Lord's Prayer, He included the idea that we will receive forgiveness for our sins AS we forgive others who have sinned against us. When we concentrate only on the offenses others have perpetrated against us, we easily overlook our own part in the problem. We can't see our reactive anger, hatred, and bitterness towards the other person. These emotions come between us and the Lord. Sometimes we blame God for the offense against us, and it drives a wedge in our relationship with our Heavenly Father.

When we choose to forgive, we release the other person from their debt against us. We let go of our end of the rope in the tug-of-war. That's not to say that what they did is acceptable or that it was without impact. Forgiveness is not approval. It isn't the same as trust either. We can forgive someone, but they may need to prove themselves worthy of our trust again. When we choose to forgive, we release our need to get even, to retaliate, or to get revenge. The Lord has said that vengeance belongs to Him. It isn't ours to seek.

Forgiveness is for us. It's to help us move forward and choose to live instead of staying stuck in the past with all of its pain. Someone who has sinned against you may never ask for forgiveness. That's between them and God. Our responsibility is to forgive so that we can live a life of freedom and abundance of soul and spirit.

The day I forgave Larry, I made the choice to forgive. It was a decision. But it was also a process. As events brought me back to the place of anger and resentment, I had to choose to forgive over and over again. It's not a one-time event. It's an ongoing act of obedience to God, trusting that He will make all things right in His time, in His way, and that He will make something beautiful out of our broken lives. When we walk in obedience, the Lord puts a song in our hearts.

Not long after that turning point in my life, He gave me the words to a poem:

A NEW SONG

*Before God gave me a new song to sing
He gave me a heart to forgive;
He took away bitterness, envy, and strife
And made knowing Him reason to live.
And now I sing a new song each day
A song full of joy and love,
A song that resounds through a once-broken heart
A song of peace from above.*

God's ways are not our ways. His ways are higher than ours (Isaiah 55:8-9). His way of dealing with offenses is to forgive. He has forgiven us our sins, and we are acting like Him and reflecting His character when we choose to forgive.

* * * * * * * *

PRAYER

Heavenly Father, help me to forgive those who have hurt me. Reveal to me things hidden in my heart, so I can release them to You for healing and cleansing. I want to please You and walk in obedience. I pray for the grace and power You've promised so I can live a life of victory and abundance. Thank You for giving me the strength to overcome every wound that's been inflicted on me. Forgive any hatred and resentment that I've been holding on to. I receive Your grace now. In Jesus' name, Amen.

A NEW CALLING

"Whether you turn to the right or to the left, your ears will hear a voice behind you, saying, 'This is the way; walk in it'."
—Isaiah 30:21

A few months before Larry left our family, we had a conversation about the ministry. By that time, he had resigned from the pastorate and was counseling to generate income.

"I don't think I was ever really called to ministry," he said.

"What do you mean, Larry?" I asked.

I think I just wanted to please my parents. I don't think I was really called to be a minister," he responded.

His words confused me. I recalled that when we were dating he informed me that he didn't want to be a pastor, but I also remembered he said he felt God tugging on his heart at the age of twelve to go into ministry.

Larry and I had been in ministry for over twenty years. However, I never had a prominent role. Wherever we served, I filled in the gaps. Now, his statements opened the door for me to question my own calling. I reflected on the struggle that night at the altar when I was sixteen years old. *Was my experience real, or had I simply responded to an emotional appeal from the pastor for young people to enter full-time ministry?*

After Larry left, there were many sleepless nights when I awoke with questions on my mind. My doubts about my own call grew. When I was a child, my father always prayed for missionaries when he said grace over a meal. He was involved with missions, and I wondered if I'd been conditioned to go into ministry as a way of getting his approval and acceptance. The questions lingered.

Was I really called to the ministry? Like Larry, was I trying to please my parents? If I was called, what does God expect me to do now that I'm alone? How can I be in ministry as a divorced woman? Why would the Lord call me if he knew I would be abandoned by my husband?

The words that Muriel Sandbo spoke over me at the women's retreat echoed in the stillness of those lonely nights. "I have called you from your mother's womb."

One night, I awoke to the same nagging question, "Was I really called to the ministry?" As I tossed in my bed, tears fell on my pillow. I couldn't see beyond my circumstances to the possibility that I could minister without a husband. I wrestled with the Lord.

"What can I do, Lord? I never finished Bible college. I don't have an education. I don't have a husband. What do You expect from me? How can I do this?" I inquired in the darkness.

As I prayed, peace came over me. I sensed in my heart that God was reassuring me of His call on my life. I needed to follow that call. The words to a contemporary Christian song by Don Moen came to my mind, "God will make a way where there seems to be no way."

"Okay, Lord. If You lead me, I'll follow. I don't understand how it's possible, but I'll listen for Your direction and walk in the path You set before me." I drifted off to sleep.

CHAPTER 11: A NEW CALLING

Within a few days, I began to investigate how I could go back to college. My transcript from Central Bible College was still in a file in my desk. I only had 63 and a half credits. I had two more years of credits to acquire before I could get a degree. The need to work during the day in order to survive obscured my vision of a future that included education. How would I go back to college? It all seemed impossible. But I wasn't willing to give up without trying.

One day, I took a personal day off from the office and brought my transcript to two local colleges. When I met with the registrars, they told me that my credits had no value and that I should save the transcript as a souvenir. Not what I was hoping to hear.

Feeling discouraged and still stuck in negative thinking about what was or wasn't possible, I went to church the following Sunday. I noticed an advertisement on the back of the Pentecostal Evangel magazine. It was promoting the Adult Continuing Education program at Southwestern Assembly of God University in Waxahachie, Texas. Hope welled up in my spirit. Maybe there was still a chance that I could finish my degree.

I took the magazine home, filled out the application requesting more information from the school, and sent it. I was accepted into the program. They accepted all of my credits from CBC and built a degree plan. But there were still a lot of questions that needed to be answered. I didn't have extra income to pay for courses or airfare to go to Texas. I needed to attend a week-long orientation so I could bring the academic material back to New Jersey and study from home. Would there be the resources I needed to move forward?

One day, soon after my acceptance, a family from my church walked into the real estate office. I greeted them.

"Hi! How are you? How can I help you?" I asked.

"We want to sell our home and find one more suitable for our family," the husband said.

"I'll get an agent. They'll be able to help you find what you're looking for."

I was about to learn that whenever I made a referral, I received a bonus. That day, I made my airfare to Texas. I made many more referrals, and every time I did, it paid my airfare. I had to fly to Texas for the beginning of each semester. Over the next two and a half years, I made six trips to Texas to work on my bachelor's degree. God made a way that I couldn't have imagined.

As the time approached for me to fly for the first time to Waxahachie for orientation, my excitement grew. For years I'd had dreams of going back to CBC to finish my degree. Literally. In my dreams, my toddler sons tagged along, suitcases and all, to stay with me in the dorm while I went back to school. My mind created the scenario to satisfy what my heart longed for. I couldn't believe it was actually happening. I was going back to college!

But before I could get to Texas, I had to live out that hot and humid day in July when I found out that Larry was gay. After that night of anguish, I wondered if I should still go. It seemed an enormous roadblock had just been placed in the center of the road I was on. I felt anxious about my sons. If I left and they found out about their father, I wouldn't be there for them. How could I go in the middle of such a horrendous time in our lives? Would I be able to think clearly or make good decisions that supported my commitment to finish my education?

I grappled with the idea of abandoning the whole endeavor. It was only one week before I was scheduled to go. Reeling from the shock and disbelief of what I had learned about my marriage, I went to the Lord and sought His peace. It came immediately. I knew I was to go, and to entrust everything to His care.

CHAPTER 11: A NEW CALLING

That week, I packed my suitcase and tried to include everything I could possibly need for the trip. I was scheduled to stay in the dormitory on campus and had to bring my own supply of sheets and towels, toiletries, hangers, everything. I didn't want to forget a thing.

The day of my flight, Larry Jr. and I got in my car and he drove me to the airport. As we pulled up to the entrance to Liberty Newark Airport, we both got out of the car and walked towards the trunk. When he opened it, it was empty.

"Where's my suitcase?" I asked, startled.

"I thought you put it in the trunk," he said.

"And I thought YOU put it in the trunk!" I blurted.

By now my anxiety level had soared, and I worried that if we drove home, we wouldn't make it back to the airport in time for my flight. We drove back to our house, put the suitcase in the trunk, and got back to the airport just in time. I boarded the plane and was off to Texas.

When I arrived at Dallas-Fort Worth Airport, a student from the college was waiting for me and drove me to Waxahachie. We arrived at the dorm, and I found the room where I was staying. When I opened the door, I was alarmed by what I saw. The room was small and contained four beds, simple wire frames with thin mattresses. All around the perimeter of the room were dead palmetto bugs with their legs in the air. They looked like huge roaches to me. My stomach churned.

I dragged my suitcase into the room and lay on one of the beds. I brought my knees up into a fetal position and cried. *Lord, what am I doing here? What is this all about?* I was alone, in a strange place, without a hint of what my future held.

After a few minutes, I went into the ladies' room. To my surprise, on the back of the stall door were the words of Bill Gothard,

"Don't be afraid of the future. God is already there." I laughed as I read these comforting words. I was sure the Lord laughed with me.

As I registered for classes, I was given forms to apply for Pell Grants. My education would be paid for. All my worrying was futile. God had everything under control and knew just what I needed.

My future was bright. He made a way where there seemed to be no way. Two and a half years later, I graduated with a Bachelor of Arts in Church Ministries with a music minor. My mother and sons traveled to Texas to celebrate with me. And celebrate we did!

****

INSIGHTS TO GROW BY

"Even on my servants, both men and women, I will pour out my Spirit in those days, and they will prophesy" (Acts 2:18).

I love the words of James Hudson Taylor, missionary to China for 51 years during the 19th century: "If you do God's work, God's way, God will provide."

When the Lord calls us to do something for the sake of His kingdom, He will provide whatever we need to do the job and accomplish His purpose. There is nothing too big for His provision and sustaining power. The Lord hears the cries of His children to supply their needs, and He is willing and able to give us what we need to do His will.

My struggle to answer God's call on my life after Larry left was in part my inability to see myself in ministry outside of our marriage relationship. I'd been in the shadow of my husband for so many years, I couldn't imagine that God would want me in ministry alone. There were few role models of women in ministry as I was growing up who didn't have a spouse to support them. Most of them were pastors' or missionaries' wives. With an impending divorce, it all seemed impossible. My desperate financial situation precluded any attempt to envision myself furthering my education and moving into a leadership role in the church.

Seeing God open the doors to go back to college and finish the education I started as a teenager caused me to rethink my stance on women and ministry. Larry had been the speaker and preacher. I spoke to women's groups on rare occasion and had spoken to a congregation only once that I recalled. The thought of being in front of groups of people terrified me. It felt too vulnerable a place, especially considering the trauma of my childhood. It involved more exposure than my comfort level could allow.

When I was told at Southwestern that I needed to take a preaching class as part of my course work, I panicked. I made an appointment with my pastor and told him I'd rather take a creative writing course and asked him what he thought of my decision. He responded, "If God has called you to preach, you won't be able to get away from it. You'd better take the preaching course." I took his words as confirmation from the Lord and reluctantly took the course, trusting God to help me do something that had previously been foreign to my mindset.

I also took a course titled, "Women in Ministry." The teaching and textbooks reinforced my understanding that God calls both men and women into ministry, and my responsibility is to follow that call. I don't need to argue my position, or convince others of its validity, but rather walk in obedience to what God has asked me to do.

On the day of Pentecost, Peter stood before three thousand people and proclaimed the words of the prophet Joel,

"I will pour out my Spirit on all people. Your sons and daughters will prophesy, your old men will dream dreams, your young men will see visions. Even on my servants, both men and women, I will pour out my Spirit in those days, and they will prophesy" (Joel 2:28-29).

God is not gender restrictive in His call to those He wants in kingdom service. As I moved forward in my call, I discerned that my inability to see myself as a woman in ministry, called and equipped by God, had more to do with my self-perception than with anything else. The messages I had received from life's experiences shouted out that I was incapable, unqualified, and unacceptable. But God assured me that He is the One I will answer to, and His approval is all I need for my life.

Our part is to follow, God's part is to provide what we need. And He can be trusted.

****

PRAYER

Lord God, thank You that You are bigger than our fears and inhibitions. You are able to give us whatever is required to follow Your call and fulfill our purpose on earth. Help us to move beyond our comfort zones and be willing to step out in faith, walk in obedience, hear Your voice, and seek only Your approval. And at the end of our lives when we stand before You, allow us to hear, "Well done, good and faithful servant." For Jesus' sake and in His name, Amen.

CHAPTER TWELVE

A NEW IDENTITY

"So God created man in his own image, in the image of God he created him; male and female he created them. God saw all that he had made, and it was very good."
—Genesis 1:27, 31

I don't remember ever hearing a sermon on the value of womanhood as I was growing up in my church. Instead, I heard sermons on how men were created in the image of God. Women, on the other hand, were taken from Adam's rib and created from him and for him. Being created in the image of God wasn't mentioned when the story of Eve's creation was taught from the end of the second chapter of Genesis.

However, my pastor's wife was very active in our church. She often led worship and taught Sunday School and women's Bible studies. Our pastor became legally blind in his later years, so she conducted services and helped him on the platform when he needed assistance. Her faithfulness was an example to us, but she was never recognized or encouraged in the area of leadership. The words "co-pastor" or "assistant pastor" were non-existent. Yet, I sensed she was just as capable as our pastor. The phrase "she knows her place" was prevalent in the sixties, and I understood it to mean that a woman dared not cross the line by moving into leadership, but had to accept her place of being in submission to men.

This experience and philosophy was reinforced in my home, and both contributed to my self-perception that I "was not good enough" as a woman. As long as I could remember, I had wrestled with negative thoughts about my value as a female.

After I found out that Larry had left me for a man, I went to Anne for a counseling session and expressed my pain and confusion at his choice.

"The rejection I feel is enormous. It's like he's saying I'm not good enough as I am, that being a woman is bad," I cried.

Anne waited a moment before speaking.

"So you were the wrong sex for your father, and now you're the wrong sex for your husband. You've been rejected for your gender by the two most important men in your life."

I looked at her and tried to comprehend what I'd just heard. My mind went blank, and I couldn't respond for a few seconds. Her statement was too threatening, too painful. I looked down at my hands, took the tissue I'd been holding in my lap, and twisted it a few times. I didn't want to acknowledge her assessment. My heart sank as I realized the truth in her words. Neither my father nor my husband could accept me for who I was.

Finally, I spoke.

"Yes. I've felt rejected in so many ways by both of them. Besides being rejected for my gender, I was ridiculed for my emotions and how I thought. I was told women are too emotional, that we over-react to life. Now that I know I was abused, I can see how I was dealing with damaged emotions. Tears came so easily. What right did anyone have to make fun of me or criticize me?"

I didn't give Anne time to respond, but I kept pouring out my pain and anger. I cried, but no longer with contempt for my own tears.

"I've been devalued by remarks insinuating that I couldn't possibly make decisions for my life. I've always felt like it would have been better to be born male. The entire time I was growing up, I wanted to be a boy. I always thought my life would have been better if I'd been born male. Now I know why I've thought and felt the way I have."

I paused and took a deep breath. I hadn't understood before our conversation how deeply I'd been wounded and the burden of rejection I'd carried for forty years.

After a few moments, my thoughts turned towards my mother.

"It's a good thing I felt loved and accepted by my mother. It would have been too devastating to be rejected by both my parents."

"You knew your mother loved you, and that was a blessing," Anne concluded.

Our session ended with my recalling comforting memories of my mother's love and gentleness throughout my childhood. I'd felt cherished by her, my grandmother, and my aunts. All the women in my family affirmed me and made me feel special. As I left the office, I sent up a prayer of gratitude to the Lord for the godly women in my life and the memories they'd lovingly created. I went home, but that night, while alone in my bed, I had a talk with God.

Am I the wrong sex for You, Lord? Did You ordain for me to be a girl? Am I a mistake? Should I have been born male? I'm the wrong sex for the two men I desperately needed love and acceptance from. Do You love me just the way I am?

I cried as I poured my pain out to Jesus. So many of my inner conflicts were brought to the surface by what I was experiencing. For all my talents and accomplishments as I was maturing, I never received praise from my father. My mother told me that he bragged about me to others, but I never heard it. I wasn't encouraged with "I know you can do it." My continual need for approval, especially from father figures in and outside the church, suddenly made sense. There was a void in the place where my person-hood, my feeling of wholeness, should have been nurtured and nourished. I was left with an emptiness that only the Lord could fill.

As I lay in the stillness of the night, I realized my entire identity had been wrapped up in being the daughter of my father and the wife of my husband. It was time to let go of my past and embrace a new identity.

I leaned over my bed, picked up my Bible, and opened it to Genesis chapter one. As I read verse 27, it was as if I was reading it for the first time.

"So God created man in his own image, in the image of God he created him; male and female he created them."

The revelation that I was created in the image of God—whole and complete as a woman—was astonishing to me. I wanted to shout, "I was created in God's image, and He said it was good!"

The Lord led me to other scriptures that reaffirmed my value as a woman. The story of Jesus' birth in Luke spoke of Mary as a woman blessed and chosen by God to bring our Savior into the world (Luke 1: 26-56). Women followed Jesus during His ministry on earth and supported Him with their own means (Luke 8:1-3). After His resurrection, women were the first to be commissioned to tell others of the good news (Matthew 28: 1-8). Mary, Jesus' mother, was in the upper room on the day of Pentecost and experienced the outpouring of the Holy Spirit (Acts 1:14).

It was a poignant moment in my acceptance of myself and my gender. In the following days as I read the stories in the Bible, especially those of women, with a new perspective, I determined to become all that I was created to be. I started to love myself as a woman and a new person began to emerge. Out of the ashes of my broken heart, God gave me a new identity, and it was grounded and rooted in Him. I saw myself as a wonderful, fearfully made creation of God. Not deficient, not less than--but a human being, loved and cherished by a God who wanted a relationship with me.

As I continued to bring my heart to the Lord for healing, the void I'd felt for so long was filled with His love. I knew I was a daughter of God, and He would never reject me. And that's all that mattered.

* * * * * * *

INSIGHTS TO GROW BY

"For you created my inmost being; you knit me together in my mother's womb. I praise you because I am fearfully and wonderfully made; your works are wonderful, I know that full well" (Psalm 139: 14, 15).

When we listen to the negative messages of the world—or some churches—concerning the value of women, we can slip into self-pity or even self-hatred. The voices we hear declare that women are not of value or worth. Or worse, that our value is in our appearance or the shape of our bodies. How it must grieve the Lord to watch us live in a constant state of striving to be good enough, to be accepted, to be valued. It must break His heart to see us slump into self-hatred, when He loved us and cherished us enough to send Jesus to redeem us from sin. While we are despising the very essence of who we are as women, God sees someone beautiful when He looks at us.

I love the words of author and speaker Liz Curtis Higgs. In her conferences she declares to women, "You are God's definition of beauty for you." That's a powerful statement. And it can be life-changing for someone who has spent their life feeling ugly.

So often, we compare ourselves to others and feel we fall short of the beauty we desire. When we position ourselves to measure up to other women, especially to the images in the media, we can miss the importance of who we are as daughters of God. When the Lord looks at us, he sees a unique, one-of-a kind woman, lovely and complete. Each of us, individually, is special to God. He knew us while we were being formed in our mothers' wombs, and His Word declares that we are accepted in all our diversity and complexity.

Since the time I was a young woman, a few decades ago, society has become more open to women in the marketplace. The number of women in college is greater than that of men. Women are allowed to enjoy activities they were banned from when I was a child. Yet, I often hear women express their inability to appreciate their womanhood. They feel cheated in life because of their gender. Their experience of being demeaned and devalued by others causes them to live in depression. They aren't able to move forward and fulfill God's purpose for their lives.

God never intended for women to live their lives regretting that they were born female. He wants us to enjoy our womanhood. He desires for us to appreciate the characteristics that make us who we were created to be by His own design. We are loving, compassionate, nurturing, sensitive, emotionally aware, and spiritually attuned. We are able to make decisions, act on them and reach our goals. We want to share power with others, not have power over them. We know the value of having influence over others, affecting their lives, teaching them what we have learned, and investing in them for the future. Women are critical to society, the church, and families. God didn't make a mistake when he created us. He knew what the world would need in feminine form and He ordained us to be. And when He was done, He said it was good. I totally agree.

****

PRAYER

Creator God, thank You for creating me just as I am. Thank You for all the beauty You see when You look at me. Forgive me for despising myself, for not appreciating all that You placed within me to bless others and give You pleasure. Thank You that You know me better than I know myself, and Your Word says You love me with an everlasting love. Help me to love myself the way You love me, and to allow Your love to flow through me to those around me. Enable me to use the qualities You've given me to make a difference in this world. I ask this in Jesus' name, Amen.

MOVING ON

"This day I call heaven and earth as witnesses against you that I have set before you life and death, blessings and curses. Now choose life, so that you and your children may live."
—Deuteronomy 30:19

As I grieved my losses, I became stuck in the pit of depression. Feelings of hopelessness awakened me each morning, followed me through the day, and continued to invade my spirit each night. Despair crept its way into my heart and mind, leaving me drained and exhausted. Nausea was constant. I felt tossed in a sea of overwhelming emotions while unrelenting storm waves crashed all around. Just when I thought I was stabilized, another event—something that reminded me of what my life had been—would dislodge my feet and push me over, gasping for air as I fell.

I continued to work at the office, doing my best to hide the turmoil I was in. But others saw the confusion in my demeanor. Some even offered their solutions to my situation. "I'm having a party on Friday night," one woman said. "I can hook you up with a young guy. You need to get out and have some fun. Why don't you come over?"

"I'm okay," I said, squeezing out a half-smile with my response. I really wanted to shout, "Oh, yeah! That's just what I need! Another man in my life while I'm still reeling from the demise of a twenty-year marriage! I'm still trying to figure out what happened!"

"You need a sugar daddy," another woman suggested. "My mother always said a little sex will make you feel better."

I'm sure my surprise showed all over my face. I felt embarrassed, and my face flushed. I looked down at the papers in front of me. I still remember my response.

"Nothing is worth my eternal soul."

Now *she* looked surprised and turned her head the other way. My words weren't meant to sound pious, but my mother had reminded me "nothing and no one is worth your eternal soul" enough times as I was growing up, that I learned to use it as my standard. I knew that when faced with life's choices, it was best to follow the Lord and not to cave in to quick choices with long-lasting, negative consequences.

There were times I felt animosity from a few of the realtors in my office. Sarcasm and smirks made me feel rejected. They wanted me to act as the world acts in times of pain and rejection. But I knew that I would reap more pain if I made ungodly choices. My sons were still watching to see if my walk matched my talk.

One day I turned to 1 Peter 4:4, "They think it strange that you do not plunge with them into the same flood of dissipation, and they heap abuse on you. But they will have to give account to him who is ready to judge the living and the dead." The Lord confirmed to me that I was right to avoid any new relationship at this point.

But as a forty-year old woman, I had temptations and desires. One day I went home, alone, to a dark house in the middle of winter, and I wrestled with God. I can still recall pulling up the driveway that evening. I turned the car off and felt like self-pity had taken over the passenger seat to keep me company. *I'll never be happy again. This is how I'll feel the rest of my life.*

When I entered the house, I closed the front door behind me. My sons were out, so I took the opportunity to let out all my frustration and pain.

"You're asking too much of me, God! This is just too hard! I can't do this! How am I supposed to do this—to obey You and Your Word? It's too hard to walk in Your ways. I was married for 20 years and now I'm alone. Won't I ever enjoy the pleasure of being in the arms of a man again?"

The Lord reminded me of 2 Corinthians 12:9 again, "...My grace is sufficient for you, for my power is made perfect in weakness."

Back and forth we went. I ranted. I questioned. Then I gradually came to a point of decision. At last, I prayed, "Okay, Lord. I hear You. Please, don't let this be for nothing. Use what I'm going through to help others someday. Help me to walk in obedience and give me the grace to do it one day at a time—one moment at a time. Teach me Your ways, Lord, teach me Your ways."

Having trusted the Lord for the strength and courage to persevere, I continued to go for therapy. My sessions consisted of Anne trying to convince me there was nothing I could have done that would have changed Larry's decision to leave. I was sure that his abandonment was based on some fault in me. I wanted to blame myself for not being a better Christian, for not being a better wife, for not being a better person. I struggled with my weight and often felt unattractive or undesirable because of the extra pounds I carried. If I changed, perhaps he would see the changes and come back to our family. It took Anne a year to convince me that what happened wasn't my fault. I wasn't in control. There was nothing I could do.

For a time, the shame of what happened felt too much to bear. The same questions pounded my mind. How could this happen?

How could I not see this coming? How could this be happening to my family? To my children? To me?

Somehow, I heard that missionaries we'd visited over the years knew about Larry leaving for the gay community. My shame was compounded. I didn't think I could live through the pain of everyone knowing. In my quiet times with the Lord, He assured me that Larry's shame was his, not mine. My shame was dealt with on the cross, and I had given it to Jesus many, many years ago. Larry's shame was between him and God.

For the first time in my life, I understood substance abuse. I knew the reason why people take drugs and alcohol to numb their pain. One day, as I drove home from my counseling session, I had the thought, *If I can hit a tree and know I would die, I could end this pain.* Deep in my heart, I didn't really want to die, I just wanted to be rid of the pain. It had been too intense for too long.

Searching the Bible one day, I came across a verse from Deuteronomy 30:19. I heard the Lord speaking to me, saying, "Choose life!" He was asking me to listen and trust Him in the midst of this storm.

There were days when my energy level only allowed me to lay on the floor, put my face in the carpet and sob my way to peace. I pleaded with God for my sons. I pleaded for my sanity and claimed the promise of 2 Timothy 1:7, "For God has not given us the spirit of fear; but of power, and of love, and of a sound mind" (KJV).

"Lord, don't let me lose my mind in all of this. Don't let my sons see me taken out of my house on a stretcher. Please, give me a sound mind. Help me to function and to walk with You each day. I feel like I'm going to lose it."

The Lord's words to me through Muriel came to me over and over again. "I will not let you falter."

CHAPTER 13: MOVING ON

How faithful of the Holy Spirit to remind me of those words! Each time they came to me, I felt I was given a teaspoon of hope.

This battle of hopelessness, shame, and self-pity continued for about three years. There were times of peace and trust. I remember sitting in the rocking chair in my bedroom, alone in the darkness of the evening, asking God to love me. I felt His arms wrap around me and the longing for security was satisfied with His very presence. And other times, I felt like I was falling into an abyss, reaching up to cling to the hem of Jesus' garment. At times I sank deep into the depression, then finally came to a place of rest. There was always a rock under me, not allowing me to disappear into the darkness. I understood that the Rock was Jesus Himself, holding me, saving me yet one more time from destruction. I thought I was clinging to Him—holding on for dear life. But all the time, He was holding me and wouldn't let me fall. I knew deep in my soul that Jesus had crawled into the pit with me and was holding me, quieting me with His love (Zephaniah 3:17).

The first glimpse of victory came one night as I lay trying to sleep. A few precious slivers of light pierced the darkness through my window blinds. As I tossed and turned, the words of a poem came to me. I reached over to my end table, picked up a pencil and an envelope. On the back of the envelope, I wrote these words:

Out of the night, the gloom, and despair,
Out of the pain and the sorrow,
Comes the Light that is shining so bright
That gives me my hope for tomorrow.

Out of the loneliness, empty and cold
Through all the days filled with care
Shines the Light who is leading the way,
Whose radiance none can compare.

The nighttime to Him is the same as the day,
His love beams through every dark place,
He'll carry me through every step of the way
'Til I stand and I look on His face.

Peace and light flooded my soul. I fell asleep and awoke the next day with renewed hope. I read over the words of the poem and titled it "Jesus, the Light." A new day had dawned. My Savior was still with me, healing my wounds and granting me another day of life.

* * * * * * * *

INSIGHTS TO GROW BY

"For the Lord is your life" (Deuteronomy 30:20).

When we're in the middle of devastating, painful, even traumatic circumstances, it's easy not to see any reason to go on living. Life seems too hard, our souls grow weary, and giving up seems like an option. Repeated losses pile up, and we feel like life is being sucked out of us until there is nothing left but emptiness. If the pain endures for years, as was my experience, it's easy to think there will be no end to the suffering. I remember feeling like there was a gaping hole in my chest that was visible to others. My grief left me feeling exposed and vulnerable. Gradually, God's unfailing love filled the void and brought healing.

The verses in Deuteronomy 30:1920 tell us to choose life, because God IS our life. He grants life to us and sustains it through His grace and provision. There is nothing we will face in this life that is greater than God's power to restore and heal. Whatever we need to be victorious is made available to us through our relationship with God—the Life-Giver.

I love the verses in 2 Peter 1:3-4 because they reinforce our hope: "His divine power has given us everything we need for life and godliness through our knowledge of him who called us by his own glory and goodness. Through these he has given us his very great and precious promises, so that through them you may participate in the divine nature and escape the corruption in the world caused by evil desires." Our Heavenly Father has given us everything we need for life and godly living. Jesus Christ secured everything we need when He hung on the cross two thousand years ago--endurance, patience, courage, wisdom, faith, resistance to temptation, peace, hope, the ability to forgive. Yes, everything!

Although there are a few who think that believers shouldn't mourn, unless we grieve our losses, we'll stay stuck and won't be able to move into the future. It's only as we grieve that we're able to let go of the past and find a new path for our lives. The words of Paul, "Brothers, we do not grieve like the rest of men, who have no hope" (1 Thessalonians 4:13), are "to be understood to mean that Christians are free to grieve more profoundly and deeply because they know that their life is grounded in God." (*All Our Losses, All Our Griefs*, Kenneth Mitchell and Herbert Anderson, Westminster Press, 1983, p.167)

If we don't grieve, we are saying that what we lost wasn't important to us or it had no meaning. When we understand that all good things come from God, because His very nature is the epitome of goodness, then we realize we need to grieve when we experience loss. "To be a follower of Christ is to love life and to value people and things that God has given to us in such a way that losing them brings sadness." (Mitchell and Anderson, p. 30) Life and all that it includes, good and bad, joy and sorrow, is to be embraced as a gift from God.

As we lay the burden of our grief at the feet of Jesus, He'll work everything we've gone through to our benefit. Another verse in 1 Peter assures us of this: "And the God of all grace, who called you to his eternal glory in Christ, after you have suffered a little while, will himself restore you and make you strong, firm and steadfast" (5:10).

It's important to remember, when we want to despair of life, that only God can work good out of evil. Our omnipotent God can take what seems like more than we can handle, even a situation that seems irredeemable, and work it for our good. Romans 8:28 says: "And we know that in all things God works for the good of those who love him, who have been called according to his purpose."

One of the ways God works good in us is to make us more like Him. We become more compassionate and more empathetic than we were before our suffering. If we allow Him to, He'll eventually use our pain to benefit those with whom we cross paths in life. "Praise be to the God and Father of our Lord Jesus Christ, the Father of compassion and the God of all comfort, who comforts us in all our troubles, so that we can comfort those in any trouble with the comfort we ourselves have received from God" (2 Corinthians 1:3-4).

As Jesus comes to us and loves us back to wholeness and makes us stronger in our faith, we can reach out to those who are hurting and offer them the comfort we've received from the Lord. There's a saying I've heard many times, and I've found it to be true: God never wastes a hurt. He uses everything for our good.

If we cling to anything other than God to find meaning in life, we set ourselves up for heartache. If we look to others for our sense of worth and value, if we live for others and they leave or die, we'll lose our reason for living when they're gone. The Lord says to choose life, because He is our life. He makes life worth living!

* * * * * * *

PRAYER

Lord, thank You for my life. Thank You that even in the darkest times, You are with me, sustaining me with Your unfailing love. Thank You that You can take everything and work it for my good. I offer up my pain, my suffering, my despair to You for Your healing touch. Help me to always choose life and to live for You alone. Please help me to comfort others in their suffering as You've comforted me. In Jesus' name, Amen.

CHAPTER FOURTEEN

A NEW HOME

"Now to him who is able to do immeasurably more than all we ask or imagine, according to his power that is at work within us."
—Ephesians 3:20

On Valentine's Day, I received a call at work from my bankruptcy lawyer, asking me if I wanted to file again to stall foreclosure on my house. I'd filed once to protect myself when Larry filed and didn't include my name. I sensed a check in my spirit that I should let it go and not file again. I would trust the Lord.

It had been six years since Larry had left. In those years, it was impossible to make a mortgage payment. I felt both terrified and embarrassed, but there was nothing I could do about it. My monthly take-home pay at the office was the amount of the mortgage payment.

By the time I got home that evening in February, I was angry. *Why do I have to bear the burden of where Ryan and I are going to live? That is Larry's responsibility. What a way to spend Valentine's Day, worrying about losing my house. This isn't fair, Lord. Not how I planned my life!*

The next few months went by quickly. Towards the end of May, I walked into the house and Ryan greeted me at the door. His face was pale and his eyes wide with fear. He had arrived home from classes at the county college to find a note posted on the front door. It was a sheriff's announcement of foreclosure to occur on August 26th.

"What are we going to do, Mom?"

"I don't know, son. I'm so sorry you had to be the one to find this notice," I said as I waved the paper in the air.

"I don't know what we are going to do. I don't have an answer. I've done everything I know to do. We have no choice but to trust the Lord."

I paused, then said softly, "He will make a way."

I hoped Ryan wouldn't hear the trepidation in my voice. I wanted to be strong for him, but my spirit was crying out to the Lord.

Eloise and Kathie, another dear friend, had met with me on a weekly basis to pray for my situation. I recall telling them that my prayer request was that the Lord would allow me to stay in my house until Ryan graduated from high school. It had been four years since he'd graduated, and I was still in the house. Our prayers had been answered, and I was grateful. But I needed a place to live and didn't know what to do.

By June I knew I had to clean out my house. I went to Allison and told her the situation. I asked her if she would fire me. That way I could collect unemployment for a while and search for a job that would pay more. I had resigned myself to the truth that the secretary position I held was not going to evolve into the administrative assistant position—and the higher salary—I'd hoped for. I needed time to figure out my next step.

I left my job at the end of June and began the emotionally and physically exhausting task of cleaning out eleven years of accumulation in my house. I planned three moving sales. Trying to decide what to keep and what to sell was draining. As I sifted through twenty years of memories with Larry, each item brought the pain of our separation back to the surface of my wounded heart. Boxes of cards and love letters mingled with tears and resentment in a pool of conflicted emotions. *Should I sell the gifts Larry gave me over the years? Should I try to keep the appliances stored? What about the toys and children's books?*

As I knelt down on the cold and dusty garage floor by the toy box my father-in-law had handcrafted for my sons, I reached in and picked up tiny cars and trucks and plastic green soldiers. Tears streamed down my face as I sobbed. I recalled older women in my church telling me my sons' childhood would go by quickly, but I had no idea it would be *that* quickly and that it would end this painfully. I sold most of the toys, but G.I. Joe,™ Star Wars,™ and Legos™ would find a place in storage. They represented too many fond memories.

My mother faithfully supported my efforts each time I had a moving sale, helping me display items, making lunch, and sitting on the porch while prospective buyers paraded up and down my driveway seeking bargains. As I followed them to answer any questions, the verse in Luke 12:15 came to my mind: "…a man's life does not consist in the abundance of his possessions." I was watching a lot of *things* I thought were important in my life be taken away by strangers. They had lost their value. And it was okay.

In the meantime, I visited the unemployment office in the next town, seeking a secretary/receptionist position. I quickly learned that I didn't have the computer skills I needed to get a better-paying job. I was unemployed and losing my house. Searching the papers for government subsidized housing was fruitless. *How would I pay the rent without a job?*

I wasn't quite ready to give up on my future. One day towards the end of July, I drove to the library at the seminary where I'd taken a few evening classes. For the past year and a half I had worked a full day at the office, dashed home for dinner, kissed Ryan good-bye, and gone to class from six o'clock until ten o'clock two evenings a week. I studied on lunch breaks and weekends, hoping to build a brighter future for myself and my sons through a graduate degree.

I walked up to the woman at the reception desk.

"Do you have any books that would tell me about scholarships for women who want to further their education?"

"Sure, they are over there. Let me know if you need any help," she said, pointing to the reference area.

I jotted down the names of a couple of foundations. I also copied a list of the scholarships the seminary offered, with the hope that I would be eligible for one of them. On the way to my car, I greeted the Dean of Students as we crossed paths in front of the seminary.

"Hi, Dean Jones!"

"How are you doing, Annalee?"

"Not well. I don't know if I'm going to be able to continue classes here. I'm losing my house to foreclosure and I don't have a job. I'm not sure what I'm going to do."

"I'm sorry to hear that. I hope things work out so you can continue your studies with us."

"Me, too. Thanks, Dean Jones. Take care," my voice trailed as we waved good-bye to each other.

I went home and immediately wrote letters of application for scholarship money through the seminary and other foundations that offered women financial support for higher education.

After mailing the letters, with one month before foreclosure, I sat at my kitchen table completely exhausted. I was running out of time. As I thought of being homeless, my heart raced and my breathing was labored. I couldn't go live with my mother. My sister and her family were living with her while saving for a new home. I felt hopeless.

What should I do? I told Ryan we would trust You, Lord. It's easier said than done!

I remembered the words of C.M. Ward, the radio preacher for Revivaltime, the choir I sang in at Central Bible College: "Desperation is always better than despair. God is never late. He may scare you to death, but He is never late."

My thoughts went back twenty years to the time when Larry and I needed an apartment for our first ministry position. I believed the Lord provided that apartment just in time. I needed another miracle! *If the Lord provided for us back then, can't He do something with this mess I'm in? Is this one too hard for God?*

As I sat at my kitchen table–the same table that had hosted ravioli dinners at my grandmother's house—I lay my head down on my folded arms and prayed silently. *Lord, if You are there, I need Your help!* A simple prayer, but the cry of a desperate child to her heavenly Father.

Two days later, as I walked back to my house after picking up the mail, I was surprised to see a letter from the seminary. *They couldn't have received my applications for scholarships so soon. What could this be?*

My hands trembled as I opened the envelope. Tears spilled onto the paper as I read:

Dear Annalee,

I am pleased to inform you that at its meeting today, the Scholarship Committee voted to grant you a scholarship.

As a scholar, you will receive full tuition remission for a total of three years or to the completion of your MDiv program, whichever comes first.

This scholarship is awarded with the understanding that your academic work will continue at the excellent level you have already maintained. The minimum grade point average required in order to continue as a scholar is a B average, and your record is considerably higher than that.

Congratulations on your strong achievements thus far, and we wish you continued success in your theological education program and God's blessings on your work and ministry.

Sincerely,

Chair, Scholarship Committee

In a flood of tears, I bent over and screamed, "Thank You, Jesus! Thank You!" Without trying to compose myself, I called my mother, brother, and sister to inform them of the good news. It was provision beyond what I could have even imagined. Through tears of joy, I shared how the Lord had rescued me and opened the way for me to return to seminary.

I later learned that that particular scholarship was only granted to new students and to those who were of the same denomination as the seminary. I was neither.

On August 24th, I moved into a one-bedroom apartment on campus and put the rest of my belongings in storage. Ryan and Larry moved into my brother's home with plans to help him with a renovation project. On August 26th—the very day they changed the locks on my house—I began full-time classes at the seminary on a full scholarship.

What a great day it was! What a miracle of provision from a faithful God! As I sat in class on that wonderful day, I choked back tears. I wasn't sure how I would manage full-time classes and support myself for the next three years. But I knew God had me where He wanted me, and I trusted His plan. His plan of provision unfolded before me.

Not long after I began classes, a fellow student asked to visit me in my apartment. I invited her for coffee, and we developed a friendship. Within a couple of weeks, she offered to help pay my rent for the first year.

I was offered jobs playing the organ for chapel and working in the library. I took a position as the resident assistant at the apartment building, resulting in a reduction in my rent. Part of my seminary education included "supervised ministry" at a local church. I received a stipend for my hours each week. People from Evangel Church sent monthly support to help pay for my health insurance costs. The Lord provided for all my needs.

Yet, I missed my sons. I visited my brother whenever possible so I could be with them. I cried all the way back to the seminary—grieving our separation, remembering how we had lived together in the house I'd just lost. It was a difficult year adjusting to all the changes. Things were about to change even more, but this time for the better.

In May, Ryan graduated with an associate's degree from the county college and Larry Jr. moved to Pennsylvania to be near the young woman he was dating. By the middle of the summer, Ryan called with good news.

"Mom, I've been accepted into Rutgers. See if you can get a two-bedroom apartment for us at the seminary." The seminary property was located in the middle of Rutgers' campus.

I secured an apartment within a few days, and by September, Ryan and I had moved in. We spent the next two years studying, working, and cooking together, and supporting each other. I typed his papers and drove him to the train station for his internship at "Good Morning America" in New York City.

Those two years will always be a precious memory for Ryan and me. Not only did the Lord provide for our material needs, but also for our emotional needs.

****

INSIGHTS TO GROW BY

"But seek first his kingdom and his righteousness, and all these things will be given to you as well" (Matthew 6:33).

When Abraham was asked to sacrifice his son, Isaac, he set out to do so in obedience to the Lord. At the last moment, God provided a ram instead. Abraham called the place where the event occurred, "The Lord Will Provide," or "Yahweh-yireh," in Hebrew. The ram was a prophetic way of showing the Lord's ultimate intention to provide a sacrifice for the sins of the world: His one and only Son, Jesus. God's provision for our sin was complete and final when Jesus died on the cross.

I'm often reminded that if our loving God provided for our salvation by giving us His own Son, he will not withhold anything that we need to live and to do His will while here on earth. Psalm 84:11 says, "…no good thing does he withhold from those whose walk is blameless." God owes us nothing, but chooses to provide all that we need, in addition to His great salvation through Jesus.

In the 1980s, a popular chorus circulating evangelical churches was entitled "Jehovah Jireh." I remember loving that chorus, and I sang it with gusto. "My God shall supply all my needs, according to his riches in glory," was a statement easy to sing when I had a husband who was providing for our family and my home was secure through regular mortgage payments.

When I was losing my home to foreclosure, it wasn't as easy to sing those words. I knew God had provided in the past, but I questioned whether He would continue to fulfill His promises. I had erroneous thoughts about God. I believed that He had only provided because I was married to a pastor and doing God's work. I wasn't sure He would provide now that I was alone and no longer in full-time ministry. James 1:17 says, "Every good and perfect gift is from above, coming down from the Father of the heavenly lights, who does not change like shifting shadows." Our lives may change, but the character of God never changes. His Word is sure and trustworthy. He will provide for all that we need.

My view of God had been too small. The day I received the letter from the seminary announcing my scholarship was more than I could have imagined. My limited perspective of what was happening in my life only allowed me a few options, and none of them were working out. God had a much broader perspective on my life, and He knew what I needed. He not only knew what was necessary to survive and thrive, but He was the only One who could orchestrate the circumstances for those things to happen. My understanding of God's compassionate provision for His children grew after I received notice from the seminary and moved onto campus.

As an added blessing, he brought Ryan and me together while we finished our degrees. The Lord knew we needed the love and support we could give to each other. He gave us favor with the housing authorities on campus to secure a larger apartment. We lacked nothing those two years.

Whatever our circumstances, our God is bigger than any obstacle that would hinder us from moving forward in His will and purpose for our lives. When we seek Him and His kingdom, He will provide!

****

PRAYER

Heavenly Father, Provider, Sustainer, Giver of good gifts, thank You for who You are. Thank You for providing my every need. Most of all, thank You for Your son, Jesus Christ, and for giving Him so freely to die for my sin. Thank You that You see the bigger picture, and You are able to do more than I can ask or imagine. Have Your will in my life, and help me to trust Your unchanging character. In Jesus' name, Amen.

CHAPTER FIFTEEN

TRIAL BY FIRE

"When you walk through the fire, you will not be burned; the flames will not set you ablaze."
–Isaiah 43:2

Seminary life was good. I felt relieved that the next three years were planned out for me. Housing was secure. I knew what was required of me, and I studied hard. Greek and Hebrew were especially enjoyable. I'd never liked studying history in high school, but church history energized me. Learning about how the Catholic and Protestant churches came into existence and the major differences between them was more than I'd previously known. Pastoral Care coursework came easily, and I soaked up all the theology courses with enthusiasm.

The atmosphere at the seminary was casual. The professors insisted I call them by their first names. I had difficulty at first, but eventually understood that we were peers, and it wasn't necessary to feel intimidated. They wanted me to succeed. The seminary's mission of training people for ministry was evident in the support and encouragement that was extended to all the students, regardless of religious background. At the time, there were over 30 denominations represented in the student body.

I made friends easily and shared openly about what I'd been through. I recall talking to one student about my circumstances.

"What brought you here to seminary?" he asked.

"I was a pastor's wife for twenty years. Then my husband left me for the gay community, and just when I was losing my house to foreclosure, I received a scholarship to attend seminary," I said.

"Oh. Can you imagine how much pain he must have been in?" he asked.

Startled by his question, my eyes opened wide and my back stiffened.

"How much pain *he was in?* He's caused enormous pain to me and my sons," I replied with my voice a pitch higher than normal.

"But you have to consider how he must have struggled. It's better that he came out. He was born that way."

I could feel my blood pressure rising and my face flushing as we continued.

"I don't believe he was born homosexual. There's no scientific evidence to support that idea. I don't see it as an acceptable lifestyle, and it certainly isn't consistent with Scripture."

"You just feel that way because he left you for a man."

Now I was angry.

"No, I feel that way because of what God's Word says," I responded.

I could see from his expression that he didn't agree with my statements. Feeling irritated and hurt by his words, I ended our conversation. I soon realized that he wasn't the only person on campus who held a different opinion than I did concerning homosexuality. Most of the faculty had accepted the gay lifestyle and promoted "tolerance" of any form of human sexual expression between consenting adults. Sex was "natural," and marital bonds didn't need to be a part of the equation.

Class discussions often went to the issue, especially in pastoral care. Part of our required reading included articles and essays that not only endorsed homosexuality, but referred to it as a way of "imagin[ing] God who is love. Homosexual love, then, becomes a way of imaging God, just as heterosexual love images God." (*Clinical Handbook of Pastoral Counseling* Volume 2, Edited by Robert J. Wick and Richard D. Parsons, Integration Book, Paulist Press, New York and Mahway, 1993, "Pastoral Counseling of the Gay Male," Richard Byrne, O.C.S.O., p. 272)

I'd become infuriated at these statements as I studied in my apartment, but I calmed myself before going to class so I could speak on the readings. I boldly argued that our society has confused sex and love. I stated that sex was not love, and it was possible to love someone without having sex with them. I added that we could have sex without loving the person we were with. I shared openly that as a survivor of childhood sexual abuse, what had been done to me wasn't an expression of love, but rather an act of violence.

Fellow students knew where I stood, and many took the same position. I wasn't prepared for what was about to happen.

After a couple of years of study, the atmosphere at seminary changed. A lesbian was hired as an interim professor. I remember walking down the hallway to see a woman coming towards me who was dressed in pants, a shirt, and a tie. I didn't know at the time who she was, but thought her outfit was strange and even offensive.

Not long after she was hired, the board of the denomination that owned the seminary fired her. There was an uproar among some of the students, mostly women. A special meeting was held in the chapel to discuss the event. Before we met, several of the male students asked me to speak on their behalf. I had been elected to serve as the Student Chaplain, and they felt safe talking to me about their experiences with the professor.

"When we're in class, she ignores the guys," one student reported.

"If I share in class, she cuts me off or shuts me down!" another said.

"Would you speak for us? We don't agree with what has happened here and that a lesbian teacher was hired without approval from the denomination."

I agreed to stand at the appropriate time and share the feelings of the students.

When the meeting convened, several female students shared their anger and disappointment that the professor had been fired. They expressed dismay at how the situation had been handled and wanted her to be reinstated.

Tension continued to build as people spoke. The room was obviously divided, not only in the physical sense that those opposed were seated on one side of the chapel and those supportive were seated on the other. But also concerning the acceptability and endorsement of the homosexual lifestyle.

There was a break in the conversation, and I took the opportunity to stand and share what the students had expressed to me. I told the administration that there were those of us in attendance who didn't see the lifestyle as consistent with our interpretation of Scripture or with our theology.

I heard several gasps. One woman seated to my right turned to me with a frown.

"And you call yourself a Christian? How is that loving?"

I was stunned and didn't answer her.

CHAPTER 15: TRIAL BY FIRE

I continued to address the administration.

"I think we should have a forum to discuss this issue. There are those who attend this institution who are gay, and there are those who have left the gay lifestyle. It would be good for us to hear both sides of the issue."

The president agreed that we should schedule a forum, and then he dismissed the students to class.

It didn't end there. I felt the glares and disapproval of some of the faculty as we were dismissed. Making my way to the ladies' restroom as quickly as I could, I went into a stall and cried. I knew I had to go to class, but I felt ostracized and rejected for expressing how I felt about the topic. I took a deep breath, prayed for strength, dried my eyes with toilet tissue, and reluctantly went to class.

Later in the hallway, a fellow student approached me and said, "You should never pastor! You don't have compassion! I hope you never go into ministry! You're intolerant!"

In my shock I didn't respond—again. These remarks came from friends I'd made over the past few years, and the reaction I received took me completely by surprise.

As I made my way towards the library to do some research that night, another student said to me, "There's a name for people like you. It's bigot and homophobe."

I don't remember my exact response, but I think I uttered something like, "I'm sorry you feel that way."

I wondered, "What happened to tolerance?" That word had been thrown at me for two years, but when I spoke up and expressed a different opinion than the administration and some of the students, there was no tolerance for *me*. There was only tolerance for those that shared their viewpoint. I felt like I was under attack. The fiery furnace of testing was getting hotter by the moment.

That night after classes, exhausted and wounded, I made my way across campus to my apartment. I wanted to escape. As I raced up the three flights of stairs, my heart felt like it would pound out of my chest. I slammed the door behind me and tossed my books on the couch. Ryan wasn't home, so I had it out with God.

"Get me out of here! You've got me in the WRONG place! I don't belong here. This is too hard. Why did You bring me here? I can't stay here!"

Too angry to listen for God's response, I went to bed, lay my head on my pillow, and cried. At that moment, I remembered what my mother told me as I was growing up: "You have as much right to believe what you believe, as others have to believe what they believe."

I cried myself to sleep that night, realizing I had nowhere to go. My home was gone. I was between a rock and a hard place. I had to stay in seminary.

The next day, while having my devotional time before going to class, I sensed the Lord speaking to me. I was ready to listen.

Turning to Proverbs, I read: "A gentle answer turns away wrath, but a harsh word stirs up anger" (15:1). I knew the Lord was instructing me. I prayed for grace and strength to face the day and obey His Word.

After my first class, I went to the cafeteria for a cup of coffee. A lesbian student came up to me.

"I think your idea of a forum to talk about both sides of this issue is good," she said.

"Thank you," I responded. "It would be better for all of us to hear from both sides."

I gave her a hug before we went to class that day. The forum never occurred. It was never scheduled.

CHAPTER 15: TRIAL BY FIRE

But I had a decision to make. How would I respond to what I'd been through? What kind of person was I going to be? I knew I had to draw on God's power to show love and respect to those who opposed me and had attacked me. I had learned that God's love was the greatest love anyone could experience—greater than any human love—and I wanted it to be evident in my life.

* * * * * * *

INSIGHTS TO GROW BY

"He guides me in paths of righteousness for his name's sake" (Psalm 23:3).

As we travel this journey called life, we will face many situations we didn't anticipate and may not know how to respond. When we least expect it, we're confronted with issues that pierce deep into our hearts and inadvertently resurrect pain we've tried to forget. In that instant, we may find ourselves at the intersection of "I'm a follower of Christ," and "Right now I want to act out of my flesh!"

When we feel judged or misunderstood, our reflex is to react defensively instead of taking a moment to think how we should respond, or if we should speak at all. Sometimes, it's better to stop and pray, "Set a guard over my mouth, O Lord, keep watch over the door of my lips" (Psalm 141:3). I've prayed that prayer hundreds of times. It has kept me from creating more pain and further damaging relationships by hurling cutting words which, once spoken, can't be retrieved.

While verbally attacked for my stance on homosexuality, I chose not to react, but to remain silent and pour out my pain to the Lord. Though I wanted to lash out at my fellow students who had stopped me in the halls and spewed their poisonous words at me, I knew that to argue with them wouldn't change their position or mine.

Instead, I decided to wait on the Lord and allow Him to work on my behalf. The previous few years had taught me that He wanted to help me walk in righteousness before Him—to choose the right path that would bring Him glory, not necessarily make me feel better when I'd been rejected. Hearing "and you call yourself a Christian" didn't cause me to question if it was true. I knew who I was in the Lord. Instead, the situation became an opportunity for others to see the fruit of my relationship with God. He promises to lead me in paths of righteousness and empowers me to take each step in His will. I wanted to remain steadfast in my devotion to God and His call on my life. To retaliate, isolate myself, or drop out of seminary may have felt easier than being vulnerable, but it would not have pleased the Lord.

So I walked the path of love, believing love triumphs over hatred. As I made my way toward love and forgiveness, bridges formed between me and those students who disagreed with me. To love and respect my fellow seminarians and professors testified to God's love that had been sown in my own heart. Secure in the love that God had shown to me, I was able to risk loving others. I had nothing to lose, and everything to gain, by walking in love.

The Bible paints a picture of love in 1 Corinthians 13:4-7: "Love is patient, love is kind. It does not envy, it does not boast, it is not proud. It is not rude, it is not self-seeking, it is not easily angered, it keeps no record of wrongs. Love does not delight in evil but rejoices with the truth. It always protects, always trusts, always hopes, always perseveres."

Treating others with kindness became a priority. I smiled and greeted everyone I saw. While working in the library, I assisted students however I could. Letting go of my anger and resentment kept me from speaking rudely.

I remember one student who continued to berate me. One day she asked me why I hated homosexuals. I saw the anger in her eyes as she confronted me. The assumption was that if I disagreed with those who accept the lifestyle, it automatically rendered me a hateful person. I felt judged again.

I assured her that I didn't hate homosexuals. I reminded her that I had lived with my husband for twenty years, and we had children together. I didn't hate him, but I hated what he'd done. Eventually, as I answered her questions without reciprocal verbal insults, her questions stopped.

For the rest of my stay in seminary, I drew on the Lord's strength and power to not only speak the language of Christianity, but also to "walk the talk." This challenged me, but in the end I became a better person, mature in Christ. I even had influence I would not have experienced had I retaliated in anger or cowered in fear.

When Job was accused by his friends of sins he wasn't guilty of, he responded: "[God] knows the way that I take; when he has tested me, I will come forth as gold" (Job 23:10). At the time of our testing and trials, the immediate discomfort seems to outweigh any possible future benefit. However, the Lord allows trials to come our way to accomplish specific purposes in our lives. As we trust Him, He broadens our understanding and creates in us the image of Jesus Christ, His Son. With Jesus—the Light of the World—shining through us, we'll come "forth as gold."

****

PRAYER

Lord God, thank You that Your love extends to every soul on this earth. Help us to live out Your love to those around us, especially when we feel misunderstood or judged. Lead us in paths of righteousness and give us the courage to stay on the path You've set before us. Bless us with grace to endure every trial we encounter. May we reflect Jesus, displaying His glory in our words and actions. For Your name's sake, we pray, Amen.

CHAPTER SIXTEEN

GRACE ON DISPLAY

"And God is able to make all grace abound to you."

–2 Corinthians 9:8

After climbing the four flights of stairs to my seminary apartment, grocery bags in tow, I opened the door; the phone was ringing. It was the end of June, and classes had concluded until the end of August. The lack of air-conditioning in the hallway on my way up had irritated me and slowed my ascent. Out of breath, I paused to lay the bags on the kitchen table, then picked up the receiver. I never expected to hear my ex-husband's voice. It had been eight years since he left. I couldn't recall the last time I saw him.

"Hi! I want to talk to you about Larry Jr.'s upcoming wedding."

"What do you want to talk about, Larry?"

By now my heart was pounding. *Why was he calling me?* Larry Jr. and Jennifer were marrying in Massachusetts, in early July. My plans were made to travel with my mother and aunt to the town where the wedding was being held. *What could he possibly want? He never calls me.*

Larry continued.

"Raymond and I want to go to the wedding together in July. We'll be staying in the same motel as you and the rest of the families. He won't attend the wedding, but I called to ask if you'd mind if he comes and we make it a vacation?"

The audacity! How dare he! I was stunned. I don't know how long I remained silent. My heart raced as I scrambled for the words to say in response to his question, without sounding hysterical. Finally, I took a deep breath and spoke in a calm, but firm voice.

"Yes, Larry, I do mind if you bring Raymond to Larry Jr.'s wedding."

"Okay. I just thought I'd ask. Thanks."

"You're welcome."

Sensing that I had just experienced God's abundant grace, I hung up the phone. Still in shock at the thought of him bringing Raymond with him to such an important family event, I sent up a quick prayer. Fearing he might bring Raymond anyway, I said aloud, "Lord, take control of the situation."

The next week, Larry Jr. called. I wasn't prepared for his request either.

"Hi, Mom! How's it going?"

"I'm doing well, Larry. Getting excited about the wedding. I have my dress and I'm packing for the trip."

"Great! I have something to ask you. It's a request about the reception."

"Go ahead. I'm listening," I said, with a gulp.

By now my stomach was in knots. I wondered if his father had called him to complain about not receiving my permission to bring Raymond to the wedding. *Is he calling with the same request?*

"At the reception, the MC will be announcing the parents of the bride and groom. I'm wondering, when they announce you and Dad, if you would be willing to put your arm in his and walk in together. I'd really appreciate that, Mom."

I took in a deep breath and slowly exhaled. My mind flashed back to last week's conversation with his father, and I was still angry at Larry Sr. for the request to bring Raymond. But I realized how much it would mean to my son to have his parents come in together, as a way of supporting him and his new bride in their marriage celebration.

"Yes, I'll do that for you, Larry."

"Thanks, Mom. I really appreciate it."

Grace flowed yet again. We ended our conversation, but the thought of being that close to my ex-husband in a public venue wasn't sitting well with me. *How am I going to do this? It feels impossible!* Gazing out the window of my apartment, I sent up a prayer: "Lord, I don't know how I'm going to do it, but give me the grace to walk into the reception hall with Larry Sr. For my son's sake."

As quickly as the prayer ended, peace washed over my soul, like an ocean wave on the sand. I knew the Lord would be with me and give me all that I needed.

July came. My mother, aunt and I arrived in Massachusetts after five hours on the road. We checked into the motel where friends and family were gathering for the big day. I felt humbled by those who had made the long trip to celebrate with us. My dear friends, Eloise and Kathie, and their families were among them.

Not long after we checked in, Larry's parents came into the lobby. They'd arrived earlier from Georgia. His mother was leading his father, who was going blind from diabetes. As they approached me, I moved toward them. We hugged and greeted each other. Then, with tears in her eyes, Larry's mother spoke in a hushed voice.

"Larry Sr. has arrived. He's staying in our room with us. He's there right now—crying."

I didn't know how to respond. But it broke my heart to know he realized this wasn't how it was supposed to be. My thoughts went to the tragedy of our divorce. There had been many times in the past eight years when I'd said to myself, "It wasn't supposed to be this way. We were supposed to be together, celebrating as a family." The words never passed my lips that night, but they stayed locked in my heart. I was determined to allow joy to override any impulse of sorrow.

After the rehearsal and dinner, we turned in for a good night's rest.

The next morning, while my mother and aunt were still asleep, I picked up my Bible for some comfort. Mixed joy and sadness still filled my heart. I needed to hear something from the Lord to assure me of His presence. I turned to Isaiah 43:18-19, "Forget the former things; do not dwell on the past. See, I am doing a new thing! Now it springs up; do you not perceive it? I am making a way in the desert and streams in the wasteland."

I knew the Lord was telling me not to allow the past to rob me of the joy of the present. It was enough to calm my soul.

Dressed in my baby blue chiffon dress with sequined jacket, I joined the others who had arrived at the church in anticipation of the union of my son and his beautiful bride.

As soon as I walked into the church, I met Larry Sr. and his parents. After greeting them, I saw my former sister-in-law, who had been standing nearby. She came up to me and put her arms around me. With her eyes full of tears, she looked into my eyes and proclaimed in a voice loud enough for my ex-husband to hear, "Praise the Lord! He has been so faithful to you! I can see His grace all over your face!"

I felt a flush creep across my cheeks. I swallowed hard, then responded, "Thank you. Yes, the Lord has been faithful to me."

I knew if I continued the conversation by telling her all that the Lord had done to this point in my life, I would cry, and my carefully applied make-up would be destroyed! So I softly kissed her on the cheek and turned around to go into the sanctuary. Grace was on display.

The ceremony was beautiful. My son wrote and sang a song to his bride. As they recited their vows, I was aware of Larry Sr. sitting directly behind me. I tried to hold back my tears, but I ended up grabbing a tissue to wipe away those that would not be denied release. My broken heart was still healing, and the wedding was a reminder of discarded vows and disregarded promises in my own life.

After the wedding, friends and family from New Jersey joined those from New England for the reception. The wedding party, parents of the couple, and bride and groom gathered in a side room to be announced. When it was time for Larry Sr. and me to walk in for the waiting guests, I took a deep breath and gently slipped my arm into his. Truly joyful at the occasion, we walked into the reception hall. I felt God's grace and strength pouring over me.

Yes! Thank You, Lord! Thank You for helping me do something I thought impossible.

At the end of the day, back at the motel, Eloise approached me.

"I saw God's grace all over you today!" she assured me.

"Thank you, dear friend! I know it was the Lord Jesus who gave me what I needed to make this a wonderful day!"

And it was.

HE LEFT, GOD STAYED

******

INSIGHTS TO GROW BY

"Those who cling to worthless idols forfeit the grace that could be theirs" (Jonah 2:8).

There are occasions in our lives that stretch us beyond what we think we are able to do. My son's wedding was one of those occasions for me. It seemed impossible for me to do what my son had asked of me. Everything in me resisted the thought of being physically close to my ex-husband, especially in a public setting. I knew my emotional limitations. Even contemplating it made me feel unsafe and vulnerable. With all I'd been through, those were the last emotions I wanted to dredge up.

On this occasion, I had to choose whether I would pray and trust the Lord for the outcome or turn to my own devices. Whether I would draw on God's grace or turn to my own idols. Idols of resentment and self-protection. Idols of defensiveness and worry over what might happen. Rehearsing conversations in my mind, preparing nasty remarks or "comebacks" if Larry Sr. said anything offensive to me. And the idol of pride. Always pride. That feeling of being stronger or more in control. The desire to show my ex-husband that I was doing very well without him, thank you.

Jonah also faced the struggle between trusting God or looking to idols. The words of the verse above are taken from the prayer of Jonah while he was inside a great fish that had swallowed him. The Lord had asked him to go to Nineveh to preach against that city because of its wickedness. Jonah knew God would save the city of 120,000 if they repented, and so he ran from the Lord, only to become dinner to a sea creature. Alone inside the fish, dark, cold, and wet, his head covered in seaweed, he cried out to God. The Lord was merciful and gave Jonah the grace he needed to be obedient to the task he'd been given. Nineveh repented.

As many times as I heard the story growing up, and studied it as an adult, I never noticed the verse above. Desperate for his life, Jonah repented of his idols of pride and selfishness. He came to the realization that any path in life, other than trusting God, forfeits the grace of God. We forfeit what only God can give us--enabling us to do what we need to do. God is more than willing to give us all the grace we need in life, and for every situation that seems beyond our abilities or decimates our comfort zone, *if we'll let go of our idols.* Anything we cling to that is not of God, not of the Holy Spirit in us, not of His sanctifying power that is transforming us, is worthless. Absolutely worthless.

When we have received God's grace in our lives, it opens the possibility of our extending grace to others. We've heard the expression, "But for the grace of God, there go I." We only need to look back over our lives to see how God's grace has made the difference in who we are and where we could have been if the Lord had left us in our brokenness. It's only by His grace that we have been saved from sin and rescued from the schemes of our enemies. When we realize this, we are empowered to be gracious to those around us and reflect the love and mercy that we've experienced.

I'm grateful to this day that God's amazing and abundant grace was given to me and my family for my son's wedding. It turned what could have been a very uncomfortable and negative event into a precious and cherished memory.

****

PRAYER

Lord, thank You for Your grace. Thank You that You pour it out to us, without measure, when we call on Your name for help. Give us wisdom to recognize our idols and turn from them. Help us to trust Your goodness in every circumstance. Give us the grace we need to bring glory to Your name as we navigate the difficulties of life. For Jesus' sake and in His name we pray, Amen.

CHAPTER SEVENTEEN

MORE FORGIVENESS

"Bear with each other and forgive whatever grievances you may have against one another. Forgive as the Lord forgave you."
—Colossians 3:13

Students, faculty, and families were seated outside in "The Grove" for Ryan's graduation ceremony. He had completed all the requirements for his degree and our family gathered on a beautiful, sunny day to rejoice with him at his accomplishment. They called each name, all twenty-four hundred, individually, so it took about two hours for his name to be read. Ryan marched across the platform and shook the hand of the college president while our family cheered. What a wonderful day! I was both proud and grateful at what the Lord had brought us through and the renewed hope we felt for the future.

I awoke one week later (at the end of May)—barely a month before my graduation—with a fever of 101.9. Strange. As an adult I never ran a fever, so I knew something was wrong. I'd had abdominal discomfort but attributed it to stress. I made an appointment with my primary care physician (or PCP as they're known), who directed me to a gynecologist. I'd just had a visit with mine, and she had sent me home with a "clean bill of health" and told me to return in a year, so I felt confused by the doctor's recommendation.

After examining me, the gynecologist sent me for an ultrasound. They found a mass the size of an egg on my left ovary. The gynecologist said he couldn't do anything about the abdominal discomfort or the results of the ultrasound until the fever was under control. So he sent me back to the PCP. The fever was continually low grade, and I became weaker as the days went by. The PCP sent me back to the gynecologist. And so it went for a couple of weeks.

I continued to work on my final papers and attend classes. I finished my last paper with a fever of 102.4. Too weak to attend my last class, I asked my mother to come to my apartment to help care for me. I lay on the couch, wondering if I had enough faith for my healing. I'd prayed for the healing of others, and I'd seen God heal family members and myself at times, but I questioned His ability to heal something that hadn't even been identified. As I silently prayed, I heard the Lord speak reassurance to me. He reminded me that as we are saved by grace, we are healed by grace. I didn't need to try to muster up enough faith on my own to be healed. I needed to rest in His unfailing love and trust Him with my life and my future as others prayed for me.

Somehow, I gained the strength to attend baccalaureate and graduation. But I was in pain. I couldn't stand upright and hobbled down the aisle of the chapel on graduation day, hoping no one would notice. Before handing out degrees, one of the faculty read the names of those who had received awards and special recognitions. I didn't expect any, and I was surprised to hear my name called—again and again. I received awards for highest grade point average, highest classroom standing for two years, excellence in pastoral care and ministerial practice, outstanding competence in Old Testament studies, and excellence in scholarship and personal growth.

CHAPTER 17: MORE FORGIVENESS

I stood and leaned on the pew in front of me each time my name was called. The words of Isaiah 58:8 came to me, "Then your light will break forth like the dawn, and your healing will quickly appear, then your righteousness will go before you, and the glory of the Lord will be your rear guard." I knew the Lord was reminding me that as I made choices to walk in His ways and seek His righteousness, He was with me. He had shown me what He can do with a yielded heart--the surrendered heart of a woman!

After graduation, my heart remained filled with joy and thankfulness at what Jesus had done in and through my life. Yet, my body continued to weaken, and I sensed that something terribly wrong was growing worse.

By the middle of July, I returned to the PCP's office. He sent me for more tests at a local hospital, where technicians reported that my white blood count was very high. The attending physician in the ER called my PCP and told him something had to be done-- soon. Finally, the gynecologist referred me to two gynecological oncologists who worked together. I called on a Wednesday and made an appointment for the following Monday.

By 1:00 a.m. on Thursday before the appointment, I couldn't stand the pain any longer. I called 911 for an ambulance and was admitted to the hospital. The oncologists came to see me and told me they'd perform surgery on Monday. By Sunday, my abdomen was swollen, and I had trouble breathing. I couldn't get out of bed.

At 11:00 p.m. on Monday, as promised, I was wheeled into surgery.

"Are you sure you want to do this at this late hour?" I asked the doctors.

They chuckled, and said, "Of course! We do this all the time!"

They performed "exploratory" surgery. A couple of hours later, they came out to the waiting room and spoke to my mother and Ryan.

"She has a 50/50 chance of surviving. The cystic mass on her ovary had grown to the size of a cantaloupe and peritonitis had set in all over her intestines. It's as if she was filled with cancer, but it's not. If you have faith, pray! If she survives, she'll be in ICU for two weeks and rehab for six weeks."

My mother and son went to my apartment and called everyone they knew. Students and faculty, friends and family, everyone who heard of my need, prayed. My brother even vowed before the Lord to fast and pray until I came out of ICU.

While I was still unconscious, a hospital chaplain that I'd known for a few years came into my room. I wasn't aware of her, but she prayed over me. She told me later that when she took my hand, I spoke in tongues. She knew I was okay when, although my body was in distress, she heard me praising God in my spirit.

How the many prayers were answered! After two days, I awoke in ICU and asked the nurses to have my mother bring my glasses and my watch.

I was moved to a semi-private room to recuperate.

Soon after, a nurse came in and asked me a question that startled me.

"How did you get these doctors to operate on you?" she inquired.

I wasn't sure what she meant, so I asked, "What do you mean?"

"These doctors are very hard to see. They haven't performed surgery in this hospital for over six years. How did you get an appointment with them?"

I smiled and said, "I think there was some divine intervention."

I knew the Lord was with me in this near-death experience. I thanked Him that His promise to never leave me or forsake me still stood.

CHAPTER 17: MORE FORGIVENESS

Recuperation was difficult and seemed long. The first week, each morning and evening, the doctors came to see me. They poured peroxide into my open wound while I held the side bars of the bed and screamed. It only took a couple of days for me to realize it would be a daily routine. When I saw the doctors appear at my door, I cried out, "Jesus, help me!"

One doctor heard my cry and said, "Yes. Jesus sent us here to help you."

After the week of excruciating pain, they stitched my abdomen. My mother came to the hospital every day to help with my care. I would awake to see her sitting at my bedside crocheting afghans. Finally, after another two weeks, I was sent home.

Once again, my mother was at my side, living in my apartment, cooking, cleaning, and caring for me. She went home after a month with the assurance that I was able to care for myself. It took several months for me to gain my full strength and heal completely.

I was allowed to remain in family housing until after the new year. By then the seminary needed my apartment for new students. A move was imminent, but there was nowhere to go. I wasn't in a ministry position because of recuperation. Working part-time for a professor brought in enough for living expenses, but not enough to launch out on my own. The only possibility of housing was to move in with my mother. My sister and her three teenaged children were already living there, and at age 50, I was reluctant to move in with my mother. Feeling confused and discouraged, I accepted that there was no other option. It didn't seem part of God's plan for my future.

Ten months after the surgery, with questions still plaguing me, I moved in with my mother. Before long, my sister found an apartment for herself and her children, so my mother and I were left to wonder why things had turned out this way. I continued to travel back to the seminary for work. After a few months, I left the job to work from home as a guidance writer for a teen magazine.

The days were filled with answering questions from teens via email and searching for a permanent ministry position. My mother and I had always gotten along, but I felt irritated with her and often left the house to walk in a nearby park. As I walked, I prayed.

"Lord, what are You doing? Have You forgotten me? Why did I go to seminary? What am I waiting for? Why did You save my life? Surely it wasn't to live with my mother the rest of my life!"

The anger grew as time went on. I caught myself snapping at my mother, and my frustration was obvious. Then, one day, while ranting in my journal, I sensed the Lord speaking to me. "Forgive your mother." I put my pen down and listened. I hadn't realized I was harboring resentment toward my mother. But the Lord revealed to me that the source of my discontent and irritation was bitterness toward my mother for not protecting me from the abuse of my childhood.

My experience with forgiving Larry had taught me that as long as I held on to my anger, I'd be miserable. If I remained contentious, my relationship with my mother would suffer, and my misery would eventually spill out to my extended family. After struggling for a few weeks, I finally surrendered to the Lord.

I determined to put my anger aside and forgive my mother. I knew she loved me unconditionally and would have done anything to protect me, especially if she knew I was being abused. I allowed my thoughts to grow into an unfair assault on my mom. I rehearsed statements over and over in my mind. "If she had protected me, I would never have made the choices I made in life and wouldn't be in this mess. It's her fault that I'm where I am."

I had developed a victim stance and blamed my mother for how my life had gone. It would have been easy to stay in that place of self-pity. But the Lord kept nudging me to forgive and allow Him to work in my life.

I whispered a prayer, "Lord, help me to forgive my mother. I know she did the best she could." A much different prayer than I'd prayed for months.

After praying, I felt more peaceful and hopeful, trusting the Lord to open the next door in my life. It wasn't in my plan to live with my mother, but it was in God's plan. Moving forward in ministry wasn't possible until I let go of the past, and everything that hindered freedom, to follow my call. Effective ministry would only emerge from a tender heart, cleansed from anger and resentment. I could remain emotionally stuck, or let go of anything that hindered me. I chose to let go.

****

INSIGHTS TO GROW BY

"But deliver us from evil" (Matthew 6:13, KJV).

It's so easy to get stuck in the past. It's even easier to get stuck on "if only." Everyone of us has something to overcome from our childhood. No one has a perfect start in life because of sin and a fallen world. We'll be wounded one way or another. We can choose to carry those wounds throughout our adult lives, or allow the Lord to heal our broken spirits.

As a mother, I know I did everything I could to protect my children from danger. But as diligent as I was, I could not completely protect them from the evil of this world. It's an impossible task. And an impossible expectation of our own parents to think they could protect us from the evil around us. So we can harbor resentment, cast blame, stay in victim mode, or allow our parents to be human and forgive them for what they weren't able to do.

In John 17, verse 14, Jesus prayed to His Father for His disciples. He said, "My prayer is not that you take them out of the world, but that you protect them from the evil one." Jesus was asking that God protect those whom He loved from Satan and his attacks. But Jesus also taught the disciples to pray, "deliver us from evil" (Matthew 6:13). Sometimes, the attacks come, and although we may never understand why God allows evil to exist, we can ask to be delivered from the aftermath and damaging effects of evil perpetrated against us.

Releasing others from our insistence that they be perfect liberates us as well. Forgiving those around us for what they couldn't stop, forgiving those who performed evil acts against us, and forgiving ourselves for the choices we made as a result of the trauma and pain of those acts, looses the grip of evil on our hearts and lives. It no longer has the power to thwart who we could have been. As we heal, we become that person we were before the evil washed over our souls. We become all that we were created to be, but with a greater capacity for compassion and love. We are able to nourish bigger and fuller souls that can reach into the hurting hearts of those we encounter who have also been touched by evil.

It takes a lot of emotional energy to stay angry. Bitterness robs us of the life force we need to change our lives. Choosing to stay in a victim mindset holds us back, and we are unable to envision the future and dream new dreams. If we allow the Lord to give us the grace we need to forgive, He'll deliver us from evil and the chains that bind us.

God is the only One who can work good out of evil. The story of Joseph in Genesis 37-50 illustrates this perfectly. Joseph was betrayed by his brothers, who sold him into slavery. He wound up in Egypt, was wrongly accused of a crime and imprisoned. But eventually he was elevated to second in command under Pharaoh. After many years, famine came to Israel, and Joseph's brothers came to Egypt seeking food to stay alive. Joseph recognized them, sent them back to Israel to get his father, and saved them from starvation. His brothers were terrified of him when they realized the man in charge was their little brother whom they'd betrayed. But Joseph reassured them, "Don't be afraid. Am I in the place of God? You intended to harm me, but God intended it for good to accomplish what is now being done, the saving of many lives" (50:19,20).

As we walk in God's ways, one of which is forgiveness, He'll work in our hearts and lives too, bringing about good from what we've experienced.

****

PRAYER

Father, we thank You that Jesus prayed that we would be protected from evil. We don't understand why evil is in this world, or why we are often targets of Satan's attacks. But we do know that You love us and You desire for us to be healed. You desire to free us from the effects of evil. Help us to forgive those who have done evil acts against us and forgive those who weren't able to protect us. Reveal to us those whom we need to forgive. We release anything from our past that would delay the bright future You have planned for us. Please give us grace to walk in Your ways and the courage to move forward in life. We ask this in Jesus' name, Amen.

CHAPTER EIGHTEEN

BEYOND MY HIGHEST HOPES

"Do your best to present yourself to God as one approved, a workman who does not need to be ashamed and who correctly handles the word of truth."

–2 Timothy 2:15

Waiting for the processional music to begin, I took my place in line in the foyer of the church and wondered how I had come to this place in my life. It was the day of my official ordination service, May 8, 2001.

Over the last several months I had passed each required exam, one lasting four hours, and had endured the nerve-wracking interviews that culminated in this special day. The road that had led to this event had been long and, at times, tested my endurance to persevere in my call to ministry. There were roadblocks and adversities to overcome. An abused childhood, a failed marriage, financial devastation, and four years of hard work for my advanced degree. I'd been through the fire and the flood over the past eleven years. Yet, I knew this beautiful spring day would birth a new path for my life, and I felt all the excitement and anticipation I'd rightfully earned.

Earlier in the day, we'd posed for individual pictures. There were seven men and two women, including myself, being ordained into church ministry. The women were presented with corsages of white roses and baby's breath. I pinned mine to the white-collared black dress I'd chosen for the occasion.

It wasn't until we lined up for the procession into the sanctuary that I felt the amazement at how much good had come out of the tragedies of my life. How could a woman who grew up believing women weren't equal to men be awaiting ordination? How was I able to overcome the belief that a woman couldn't be a spiritual leader? I remembered all that I'd been through and the healing God had brought into my life by the power of His love. I stood in line with a heart bursting with gratitude. I'm sure my face beamed and my eyes had an inner glow obvious to the others as we waited to enter. This was beyond what I ever hoped for during the darkest hours of my life.

It was also the moment it became apparent that I was the only person without a spouse to accompany me down the aisle. All the other candidates had marriage partners.

As the music began, we moved slowly and steadily down the aisle. I was last in line. But to my surprise, I didn't feel alone. I remembered the words of Isaiah 54:5: "For your Maker is your husband—the Lord Almighty is his name." I smiled at the family members and friends who had gathered as I moved toward my seat in the front row with the other candidates.

After a time of singing and worship, the national Assistant Superintendent, Dr. Crabtree, stood up to preach. He concurred that this night was the culmination of years of preparation. He emphatically reminded us that we couldn't be ordained without proving ourselves fit for ministry.

Dr. Crabtree preached a riveting sermon from 2 Timothy. He admonished us to live a sanctified lifestyle in a corrupted culture: "It's everybody's business if you sin. When you're tempted to sin, ask yourself what it will cost you. You're not in the ministry for yourself, but for others. God has entrusted you with the Gospel. If you sin, you'll have to live with the consequences. No minister should carry the burden of sin with the burden of ministry. It's too much to bear. It is your family's business if you sin. Your family is at stake. It will affect you, your marriage, your children and your grandchildren. It's the church's business; people will be grieved and brokenhearted. And it's the world's business. They're looking for someone who will live what they believe. Someone who is honest and does what's right. When they're in trouble, they'll come to a person of God. So die to sin and come alive to God and the gospel."

He told the story of a fellow leader who called him to share a recent experience. The leader told Dr. Crabtree that he'd just come from the home of one of the pastors in his district. When he entered the house, it was his job to tell the wife that her husband was, at the very same time, being confronted in the district office for his immorality with someone in the church. The wife fell to the floor with a scream and crawled across the room on her hands and knees.

I could relate to the crushing pain of the woman he was telling us about. I knew firsthand what it felt like to be devastated by your husband's choices and to feel like your whole world had just crashed and burned. I knew what sinful choices could do to a marriage, to a family, to a church. I sent up a silent prayer for the wife, asking for God's mercy on her in her pain.

Dr. Crabtree continued: "Remain in a wholesome relationship with God by renewing your faith and relationship with Him each day. Remain in a healthy relationship with your family. Practice what you preach. Your children will see what you do in your home. It won't matter what you do in the pulpit. Maintain a wholesome relationship with your church. Do what you've committed to do with joy. And keep an honorable relationship with the world. Pay your bills! Keep a good reputation with the world."

Then he spoke very specifically about our responsibility as ministers of the gospel of Jesus Christ: "Have a scriptural orientation at this time when the authority of the Bible is under attack. Be a preacher of the gospel, not theory or philosophy—but the Word of God! There's only one way to heaven. If there was another way, we'd be confused."

The congregation chuckled at his sense of humor.

"We are only saved through Jesus! There's healing in the Word! You're here to declare to others the saving and healing power of Jesus. He is everything people need."

He had our complete attention. At times we applauded. At times he paced back and forth, and at one point he came down from the pulpit and was in the aisle, fervently sharing his heart with us: "Allow God to interrupt your agenda with glorious surprises. Believe that signs and wonders will follow your ministry. Believe that you have more power in you than all the devils in the world! Don't allow people to walk out of a service the same way they walked in. Preach Jesus and leave the results to God."

We knew he was telling the truth! We sensed the Spirit of God in our midst. The entire congregation spontaneously stood to its feet and applauded his words when he concluded the sermon. It was a powerful message to those of us taking not just another small step in our lives, but a leap of faith to follow our call.

After another time of corporate worship the District Secretary, Rev. Spinola, came to the pulpit and introduced the candidates to the congregation. He reminded us that we'd given ourselves to the preparation of meeting all the criteria for the call of God as well as the standards of the Assemblies of God. He asked us to step forward at the appropriate time.

When my name was called, I stood up and took my place with the others at the altar. Rev. Spinola reiterated to us the seriousness of our call and admonished us to determine to live in a way pleasing to God.

I bowed my head and prayed silently.

"Lord, give me the strength and courage I need to follow Your call. Help me to be faithful and not be enticed by the world and all it has to offer. Lead me in paths of righteousness. Help me to guard my heart and never, never bring disgrace to the cross."

The words Muriel spoke through the Holy Spirit years ago at the retreat in Pennsylvania came to me. "I have called you from your mother's womb. I will not let you falter. You are graven in my hand."

Rev. Spinola's words rang out over the candidates as we prayed.

"Maintain the dignity of this high call of God on your lives. Remain faithful to the call and to the ministry."

My thoughts flashed back to Larry's ordination service many years before in Michigan. How he and his mother hugged and cried at the joy of his accomplishment. I thought of prominent leaders who had fallen and all those who went down with them.

My heart cried out to God, "I have clay feet! Don't let me go down the same road! Give me the grace I need to one day stand before You and hear, 'Well done, good and faithful servant.'" My tears dripped on the altar before I could catch them in my tissue. I prayed quietly in tongues, pouring my heart out to Jesus.

Then Rev. Spinola asked, "Do you promise to give yourself wholly to the ministry and lift high the name of Jesus? If you accept this charge, say 'Yes, with God's help, I do.'"

I joined the other candidates in responding, "Yes, with God's help, I do." And I added in my heart, *With everything that is within me, I promise to give myself to You and bring honor to the name of Jesus.*

At this point, we were presented with our Bibles. The waiting spouses joined their partners at the front of the room. Once again, I stood alone. But only for a minute. My former pastor's wife, the only one I'd known for the first twenty-four years of my life, came to my side and stood with me. I'd asked her to come to my ordination and stand with me during the time of prayer. She was close to eighty years old, and my mother had arranged for her to be escorted to the church that night. I felt honored and proud that she had come.

Rev. Spinola laid his hands on my head and ordained me to the full gospel ministry "in the name of the Father, Son, and Holy Spirit." Then he prayed over all of us: "Lord, use them; pour out Your Spirit on them. Set them apart for a lifetime of ministry, in Jesus' name."

As prayers continued, a soloist on the platform sang, "In Christ Alone I Place My Trust." I wiped my tears and prayed silently that I would continue to trust the Lord in whatever He had for me to do in this sacred calling.

A final prayer was offered, and then Rev. Spinola placed a handmade, blue-and-white satin mantle on my shoulders. It was embroidered with a cross and dove on the front panels. My initials were embroidered at the neck along with the date of my ordination. The mantle was a reminder of the honor bestowed on each of us and a symbol of the challenge to serve God and His people in purity and integrity.

A former District Superintendent was asked to come to the platform and close the service in prayer. I lowered my head and smiled to myself as he approached the platform. I flashed back to nine years earlier when I'd sat in his office.

"I sense the Lord has called me to the ministry, and I want to be credentialed in the New Jersey District," I had shared with him.

He had smiled, glanced at the floor and tilted his head as he replied, "Well, this district isn't very open to women in leadership.

I'd advise you to forget about being credentialed here. Maryland is more open to women in ministry. It would be better for you to seek a teacher's degree and teach in a Christian school if you want to stay in New Jersey."

I recalled thinking, "We'll see about that. God's not done with me yet!"

My ordination was a blessed time for me. A time of reaffirming my call to ministry. A moment of recognizing the greatness of God and what He can do with a broken vessel. A season of finding rest in the sovereignty of God.

To close the service, the priestly blessing from Numbers 6:24-26 was given:

"The Lord bless you and keep you;

The Lord make his face shine upon you and be gracious to you;

The Lord turn his face toward you and give you peace."

When the recession music began, I left the sanctuary with the other newly-ordained ministers to see a dear friend from seminary who had surprised me with her attendance. We hugged tightly and cried together. Many mornings during our seminary years we'd met in the chapel and prayed together, ending our prayers with the Lord's Prayer.

Now both of us had been ordained. Our prayers had been answered.

"Thy will be done on earth as it is in heaven."

****

INSIGHTS TO GROW BY

"And I will restore to you the years that the locusts hath eaten" (Joel 2:25 KJV).

During the most painful times of my life—reliving the memories of abuse, the abandonment and rejection—I often wondered who I could have been if I'd had a different life. I mourned over what I'd lost and grieved the person who was robbed of her personhood, of her potential, of her possibilities. I often considered how the emotional damage I'd suffered and the resulting fear and anxiety had thwarted who I might have become. If I hadn't been so fearful, could I have accomplished more? If I'd been stronger, would I have had a more positive influence on others? But during what seemed like endless hours of asking "what if," the Lord was preparing a future I couldn't have imagined.

The night of my ordination was an enormous part of the healing that God brought into my life. I not only survived-- but thrived-- in spite of the horror and devastation of the past. The broken pieces of my life were reassembled by the Master Painter who created something more beautiful than I could have painted on the canvas of my own life. The Spirit reaffirmed to me that we don't have to be defined by our past; our identity doesn't need to be tethered to our painful experiences. Our identity is in Christ Jesus, and that overrides all other labels placed on us by ourselves or others.

In my prayers over the years, I'd asked God to restore to me what I'd lost—what had been taken from me. In essence, I asked Him to help me become all I was created to be before the trauma of being violated. I knew it was asking for the impossible from a human perspective. After all, we can't go back in time and live our lives over again. We can't recapture something like childhood innocence or trust. But *there is* healing, and when God restores to us what has been stolen, He does it completely. I knew in my heart that He would use everything I'd endured to touch others. God doesn't waste a hurt. My ministry would come out of my pain.

The verse above is from the book of Joel, an Old Testament prophet. An invasion of locusts had stripped bare the land of Judah, and the people were left devastated on every level of their existence.

Being an agrarian society, their livelihood depended on the land producing crops for food and commerce. But locusts had utterly destroyed the vineyards, trees, and fields, creating great suffering for the inhabitants. There was no hope left. Only despair.

In the words of Joel, who spoke for God, he promised that if the people sought God, He would restore to them what the locusts had eaten. The Hebrew word for "restore" has a broad meaning. According to Strong's Exhaustive Concordance of the Bible, the word comes from a root word meaning "to be safe (in mind, body or estate)." Strong goes on to say it can also include phrases like "to make complete, to make full, give again, re-pay, make to be at peace, prosper, make restitution and reward."

From the initial call I sensed as a teenager, to the place of becoming ordained, felt like all these things to me. I was no longer plagued by fear but felt safe and at peace. A sense of destiny overwhelmed me. Nothing had been lost—only delayed until the right time. I felt restored to a place of wholeness. To a place of calm in the knowledge that God was ultimately in control of my life. What I'd been robbed of had been returned to me, but with greater richness and depth. As the Psalmist did, I testified to God's goodness, "The boundary lines have fallen for me in pleasant places; surely I have a delightful inheritance" (Psalm 16:6). My life was fuller than it would have been without the suffering.

I was complete in His hands. The shattered pieces had been remolded into something beautiful and holy. There was no longer room for wondering what I could have been. I had become what God intended for me to become. Instead of merely surviving, I had thrived. And so can you.

* * * * * * * *

PRAYER

Lord, help us remember that You aren't done with us yet. You are completing the work You began and will continue to restore all that has been taken. You will not allow the enemy to destroy us but will protect and give us everything we need to become all You want us to be. We ask for patient endurance when we become fearful and can't imagine what our future will hold. Remind us that You hold the future in Your hands. It belongs to You. In Jesus' name we pray, Amen.

CHAPTER NINETEEN

THE GOD OF SECOND CHANCES

"He has made everything beautiful in its time."
–Ecclesiastes 3:11

" For Heaven's sake, Annalee, you're just going on a date. You don't have to marry the guy!" My sister's words rang in my ears as I hung up the phone. As we talked, my voice had displayed the anxiety of a schoolgirl. She assured me that my first date with Joel would go well, and that I shouldn't worry. Easy for her to say. By this time, it had been twenty years since I was abandoned, and I had lived alone for twelve years. The idea of dating at fifty-three years old made me uneasy. Would I know how to act? How would I respond if he tried to kiss me? I'd called my younger sister for some reassurance.

Actually, Joel and I had been getting to know each other for quite some time. We first met when I came to his church as a guest speaker. After the service, we chatted over a cup of coffee. Six months later I took a job with the church as an assistant pastor, my first ministry position, and moved into a townhouse, which as it turned out was only a half mile from Joel's home.

Part of my responsibilities included leading worship. I played the keyboard, and two other church members provided drums and bass guitar. Joel was a gifted musician, and when I asked him to be our acoustical guitarist on the worship team, he agreed to play.

Every Wednesday evening the musicians gathered in the basement of my townhouse to practice for the Sunday service. Often, after the others left, Joel and I lingered. We'd pray together. He had gone through abandonment and divorce seven years prior, and we had a lot in common. We related our experiences of walking through life with faith in God. I liked his honesty and sincerity. He drew me with his transparency and sense of humor. He spoke with clarity and had a wonderful vocabulary that added to his appeal. I learned later that he had a degree in English.

I looked for opportunities for us to be together.

One summer evening, I planned to attend a singles' dinner sponsored by our church. I carefully chose the outfit I would wear, hoping Joel would notice. Everyone was asked to bring a contribution to the meal. Joel brought cheesecake with blueberry sauce that he'd made himself. A man who cooks. I was impressed!

After our meal, we played croquet, and everyone else finished the game but me. Embarrassed, I kept hitting the ball in an attempt to finish, but Joel didn't seem concerned. He stood by yelling, "It's Annalee's turn!" With each stroke he'd repeat, "It's Annalee's turn!" I roared with laughter. I knew then that I was falling in love. I also knew that I was fighting my feelings. Trusting someone enough to be in a serious relationship again seemed like too much of a risk.

It had been eighteen months since I first met Joel, and I was becoming more and more attracted to him. Besides all his talents and character traits, I thought he was really cute! I didn't learn until later that he was attracted to me and was having similar feelings. He was fighting his feelings just as hard. After his divorce, he had resigned himself to staying single and going into ministry.

I had done the same. There was no room for falling in love. I often woke in the middle of the night with Joel on my mind. I tossed and turned, commanding my heart to stop feeling anything for him. I couldn't stop the dreams of what our future could be together. In the darkness, questions forced themselves into my consciousness as I lay in my bed.

How can I ever trust another man? How will I know if he's authentic? How could this ever work?

Then, one autumn day, I expressed to Joel my disappointment over a cancelled trip to New York City. Some friends had invited me to go to Manhattan with them, but their plans changed. I love the Big Apple, and it was fall—my favorite season. I yearned to go.

"I'm thinking of going into the City anyway," I mused. "Maybe I'll go see '*Madame Butterfly*.'"

"By yourself?" Joel asked.

"Yeah. Why? Do you want to go?"

I paused for a moment. Did those words just come out of MY mouth?

"Sure, I'll go with you," Joel quickly responded.

"Do you like Puccini?" I asked.

"I don't know. I've never seen an opera."

"Well, that settles it! You must see an opera. I'll go online for tickets and see what's available for Saturday."

With a crispness in the air and the leaves in their splendid array of colors, Joel picked me up for our trip to the City. When I answered the door he blurted, "Look at you! You look terrific!"

Yes! I thought, trying not to act excited that he'd noticed. I was wearing a dressy black and white pantsuit that seemed to fit the occasion.

In the car, we shared our excitement over seeing the opera, and I inadvertently made a remark about being on a date. "Is this a date?" Joel inquired, almost gasping. He hadn't been on a date for thirty-three years, and at fifty-four years old, he was just as nervous as I was to be having an official romantic encounter.

When we arrived in New York, we enjoyed a delicious meal "al fresco" at a restaurant across the street from Lincoln Center, where we would be viewing *Madame Butterfly*. With an hour to spare before curtain time, we walked up Broadway to a record store. There we searched for a specific version of *Handel's Messiah* that Joel had been looking for. In the display case was the CD he wanted. He looked at me in amazement and said, "I've been looking for this for years!" Our eyes met, and we knew we had both found something we had searched for --but had only dreamed of experiencing.

The New York City Opera offered a magnificent production of my favorite opera, and we savored every note. As *Butterfly's* aria "Un bel di" (One Fine Day) floated up to our fourth-tier seats, we glanced at each other in wonder at the beauty of the music—and the moment. When it was time to leave, we took advantage of the balmy, autumn evening and walked up Broadway once again. This time, Joel offered me his arm. We joyfully walked arm in arm, lingering in the magical feel of the night.

When we arrived in our hometown, it was well past midnight. We'd talked all the way home and then, suddenly, there was a lull in our conversation. I took the opportunity to tell Joel how much I enjoyed getting to know him, and that I valued our friendship. His response was simply, "Really?"

"Yes," I continued. "It has stirred some feelings that I didn't think could be stirred again."

Joel, "Mr. Vocabulary" as he was known, glanced at me while still driving and said, "Really? What kind of feelings?"

CHAPTER 19: THE GOD OF SECOND CHANCES

"Deep feelings. I've been waking in the middle of the night for about three weeks thinking of you."

"REALLY?" was all Joel could get out, in his shock at my confession.

Then he added, "I've been doing the same thing, Annalee. I've been waking up thinking about you."

By now, we were in front of my townhouse. Joel stopped the car and turned towards me.

"I'm in love with you, Annalee."

"I'm in love with you, too, Joel."

He leaned towards me.

"May I kiss you?"

"Yes!"

After we shared a tender kiss, Joel asked, "Will you marry me?"

I looked down and thought for just a moment, *I can't believe he's asking me this. There hasn't been anyone else in twelve years that I would consider marrying.*

Then I looked up at him and replied, "Yes. I'll marry you."

That night we pledged our love to each other.

The next night I called my sister.

"Guess what?" I asked.

"What? What happened on your date?"

"Joel asked me to marry him, and I said yes!"

I heard my sister scream on the other end of the line.

"You did what? Are you crazy?"

"No. Seriously. He proposed, and I said I would marry him. We love each other. We've really been getting to know each other for about a year and a half. We're getting married."

It was my turn to reassure my sister that everything would be okay.

By Monday afternoon I had picked out my wedding gown of ivory satin and lace, sprinkled with pearls and sequins. The next six months were filled with planning, Shopping, and making sure all the details were arranged for our wedding.

We celebrated with a large wedding attended by friends and family. My sister was my matron of honor. Three dear friends served as bridesmaids. Joel wrote and sang a song titled "Healing Love" based on Song of Songs 2:10-13:

"My lover spoke and said to me, 'Arise, my darling, my beautiful one, and come with me. See! The winter is past and gone. Flowers appear on the earth; the season of singing has come, the cooing of doves is heard in our land. The fig tree forms its early fruit; the blossoming vines spread their fragrance. Arise, come, my darling; my beautiful one, come with me.'"

During the ceremony the congregation sang the chorus titled "In His Time." God had indeed made our lives beautiful in His time. As we exchanged vows, we rejoiced in the love we'd found in each other.

At our reception, we danced the afternoon away. Yes, we had an afternoon wedding, because we had reservations to see an opera at 8:00 on our wedding night. After seeing *Butterfly*, we had purchased season tickets to the opera, and the last scheduled performance of the season was on the night of our marriage ceremony.

Following our reception, we drove into the City--where it all began. We checked into a hotel across the street from Lincoln Center and made our way to our seats to see *La Boheme*. I was wearing that same black and white pantsuit that I'd worn on our first date. Only this time, I had baby's breath and silk flowers from our wedding in my hair.

We held hands as we listened to another love story by Puccini. We had begun our new life together as husband and wife, remembering "one fine day"—when good friends began their journey as lovers for a lifetime.

****

INSIGHTS TO GROW BY

"Though you have made me see troubles, many and bitter, you will restore my life again; from the depths of the earth you will again bring me up" (Psalm 71:20).

Allowing myself to have feelings for Joel was frightening after what I'd experienced in my marriage. Divorce had been much too painful for me to take the risk of being in another committed relationship. The rejection and abandonment had crushed me. The scars went deep. A wall of protection had gone up, and I had convinced myself that it wasn't possible to trust again. In my mind, staying active in ministry and single for the rest of my life was the only option that secured a future without repeating the pain I'd endured in the past.

However, God had a better idea. He knew the plans He had for me, and they included marriage to a man who loved Him and me. God wasn't limited by my pain or fear. His plan wasn't thwarted by my pessimism or skepticism.

He can work in our lives to restore the things we've been robbed of, if we let Him. He is able to mend a broken heart. He can breathe life into a callous heart and resurrect a desire to be in a loving and trusting relationship again. He isn't limited by our human weaknesses. Nothing is too hard for Him.

One obstacle I faced in moving toward a new relationship was my questions and erroneous beliefs. Questions like, "How will you know if the person is telling you the truth?" Beliefs like, "You can't trust your own judgment to be in another relationship." These and many other statements filled my mind for years.

By allowing the Lord to speak the truth to my heart, I slowly opened the doors that had been bolted shut to allow another person into the deep places. God brought scripture verses to my remembrance that assured me that He could do the impossible. I read verses that told me He wanted to restore to me the things I'd been robbed of and had been taken from me. I reviewed Romans 8:28, where God promises to work out all the events of our lives for our good.

In their book *Telling Yourself the Truth*, William Backus and Marie Chapian write, "'Perfect love casts out fear' "(1 John 4:18) means to us that the love of God has wiped out the power of fear over our lives if we will use God's methods of conquering it. 'Cast your fears [cares] on Me!' He explains, 'Give them to Me! I know what to do with them.' It is in this way we are set free to take risks. Then whether we succeed or fail is not our utmost concern. We are not enslaved by fear of negative results. Painful fear and anxiety no longer play a dominant role in our lives." (p. 133, Bethany House Publishers, Minneapolis, Minnesota, 1980,1981,2000)

I had to overcome the fear of what others would think if I remarried. There are those who understand that divorce isn't always avoidable. They can accept that there are victims in divorce situations. But remarriage is another issue. Many sincere Christians and churches prohibit remarriage under any circumstances—even abandonment.

Knowing that God's love for me was not diminished by my divorce, and that His love would carry me through every circumstance of life, allowed me to take the risk of loving and marrying again. Joel and I had both come to a place of willingness to risk loving each other and allowing the Lord to take care of those who might oppose our marriage.

There are no perfect people, and there are no perfect marriages. But we love and serve a perfect God who is able to take what was once a painful and destructive experience and turn it into a new and restorative adventure. He's the God of second chances!

****

PRAYER

Heavenly Father, thank You for Your steadfast love. Thank You that You pick up the broken pieces of our lives and weave a new and beautiful tapestry that brings glory to Your name. Help us to be willing to take the risks that are within Your will and leave the results to You. We never have to fear being rejected by You. And for that we praise Your name. In Jesus' name we pray, Amen.

CHAPTER TWENTY

BE STILL—AGAIN

*"For I am convinced that neither death nor life, neither angels
nor demons, neither the present nor the future, nor any powers,
neither height nor depth, nor anything else in all creation, will
be able to separate us from the love of God that is in Christ
Jesus our Lord."*
–Romans 8:37-39

It was mid-December and the unusual winter weather sent a
brush of warm air across my face. A few remaining autumn
leaves swirled around me and crunched under my shoes as I walked
towards Walmart. It was much too warm in New Jersey this season,
and I'd had a hard time getting into the Christmas spirit. But that
day I was determined to do some shopping.

As I walked towards the front entrance to the store, my cell
phone rang. I scrambled for it in my over-sized, over-filled purse and
took the call. It was my daughter-in-law, Jennifer, Larry Jr.'s wife.
She was calling from Maine where they'd taken a pastoral position.

"Dad is missing," she choked through her tears. "Aunt Jane
called and said she dropped him off at work two days ago and he never came home. They don't know what happened to him. He didn't

take any clothes or medications."

As I heard Jennifer cry, tears filled my own eyes. I walked back to my car, and with clammy hands, reached for a tissue. Searching for words to comfort her, I lowered my voice in an effort to not burden her with my fears.

"I'll pray, Jen," I assured her. "And I'll ask others to pray, too. We have to trust the Lord with his life. Please keep me posted. Call me if you hear anything." She promised she would.

By this time, Larry had moved back with his mother in Georgia. My sons had only occasional contact with him. It had been almost seventeen years since he left, but about two years since I'd seen him. I still prayed for him. My fasting and praying for all those years had centered on the desire to see him return to his relationship with the Lord and be reconciled to his sons and family members. Now those prayers seemed to have been in vain. *Was this his end?*

Fear and anxiety surfaced. *What could have happened to him?* Immediately my thoughts went to suicide—or murder. I had no idea how he had been living and was terrified at the thoughts of what might have happened.

I grieved for my sons. I didn't want them to have to endure more pain from their father's actions. I wondered if they would ever hear from him again. I shuddered at the thought that they would have to bear the burden of never knowing if he was alive somewhere or, if he had died, how it had happened.

I cried out to God, "Please, Lord, have him contact someone. Don't let him be dead without us ever knowing what happened to him."

The holidays came and went. It was unusual for my sons to not hear from their father at all. He always called or sent a card to stay in touch with them at Christmas. This year they heard nothing.

CHAPTER 20: BE STILL—AGAIN

Everyone around us prayed. Joel and I prayed together. Finally, I asked the Lord to please let us know one way or the other if he was alive or dead so there could be closure. Not knowing was taking its emotional toll on all of us.

Then on January 25, I received a call from Larry Jr. in Maine.

"I just answered a call from a social worker in Miami. I'm trying to get in touch with them now. They said Dad was admitted to the Alpha and Omega Hospice there, and he gave them my number. I'll call you as soon as I find out what's going on."

I hung up the phone and called a dear Christian neighbor whom I had shared with a few nights before about what we were going through. The next day she came to my front door with chicken soup, a loaf of bread, daffodils ("For new life," she said) and a note. I hugged her and thanked her for her thoughtfulness as she left.

After bringing the soup into the kitchen, I opened the card to read, "Be still and know that I am God" (Psalm 46:10). I let out a deep sigh, suddenly remembering what the Lord had spoken to me 17 years prior. He was asking me to trust Him once again.

My son called back that evening.

"Mom, you'd better sit down for this."

My son reported that Larry Sr. had been in Miami to start "a new life." He became ill and went to an emergency room where he was X-rayed. The test showed four or five large tumors in his lungs, and the doctor had given him two or three months to live.

Larry told me he wanted to go to his father as soon as possible. I knew we would have to do whatever it took for my sons to get to their father. I wanted them to see him before he died. I wanted them to know if he'd given his heart back to Jesus. I wanted them to hear "I'm sorry for what I did and all the pain I caused you." I knew what I wanted-ed. They were all good things. And I would help to see it happen.

"Did you tell him you loved him?" I asked before we ended the conversation. "Yes, and he cried," my son shared. I felt relief that Larry's heart had softened to the point of tears, and also that he knew he was loved.

The next couple of days we talked back and forth about getting my sons to Miami. Larry's mother and sister were now in touch with him, and they were trying to get there, too. The more we tried to make plans, the more impossible the situation became. By now it was a week before Super Bowl Sunday to be held in Miami, and there were no motels under $300.00 a night. Airfare was also high. Everyone was trying their best to get to Miami, but it was taking a few days to figure out the logistics.

In the meantime, it was my turn to preach on Sunday evening at the church my husband and I were planting. The Lord directed me to Psalm 46–the "Be still" Psalm. While studying, I had learned that the Hebrew word for "still" can also mean "let go." Verse 10 can read: "Let go and know that I am God." I prepared to preach and knew my message was from the Lord.

Saturday morning, Larry Jr. called with an update. "He's getting weaker. He said he's in a wheelchair and he can't keep food down. Are you willing to come to Maine to take care of the girls? When would you be free to come?" my son inquired. By now I had three lively granddaughters.

"Let's see what flights are available," I replied. We looked at the possibilities online, but my mother was also coming, and she didn't feel like she was ready to leave for a couple of days. I had hesitations about traveling before the weekend because of plans I'd made months prior. We decided to try for early the next week.

Sunday morning, Joel and I headed to Evangel Church. I'd heard that Don Piper, the author of *Ninety Minutes in Heaven*, was speaking. I was excited at the prospect of hearing him. I'd attended a writer's conference that past August and sat under the teaching of the man who helped Don write the book, Cecil Murphy. So, I felt a connection with the authors.

We took our place for worship and sat in quiet prayer, waiting for the service to begin. I could feel tears slowly running down my face. This was the last place Larry and I had ministered together. It was my home church. Anyone noticing would recognize the scene. For several years after Larry left, fellow congregants watched as I sat through the services, broken and grief-stricken. I recalled many times when I couldn't lift my voice to sing. All I could do was cry. This particular Sunday, my emotions were in high gear once again.

As we sang, I prayed and worshipped at the same time. *Please, Lord, let him stay alive until they get there. Please, Lord, have mercy on us.* Across the screen for the worship songs came the words, "Be still and know that I am God." *Okay, okay, Lord, I'll trust You with this whole thing. I get the message! Thank you for working this out and answering my prayers.*

After the service, I purchased a book and asked Don Piper to sign it. Then I asked him to pray for Larry and what my family was going through. After he prayed, I had a deeper level of peace. Then the pastor came up to me, having heard about Larry, and offered for the church to pay airfare to Miami for both my sons. My heart leapt with praise. *Thank You, Father! I know You are working in this situation and You have it under Your control!*

That night I preached, knowing that the Lord was guiding us and taking care of us. I needed to "Let go and let God."

On Wednesday, my mother and I flew to Portland. Larry picked us up at the airport, and we arrived to see three beautiful blond-haired girls giggling and jumping. We were excited to be together, no matter what the circumstances.

That evening I spoke to Larry Jr. before he and Jennifer left Portland.

"When you get down there, I want you to give your father a message from me. Tell him I forgive him. That's all. Just that I forgive him."

"Sure, Mom. I'll tell him," Larry said.

Larry and Jen headed to the airport, where they would stay overnight for their 6:00 a.m. flight to Ft. Myers. They planned to stay there at Jennifer's mother's vacation home and drive across Florida to Miami on Thursday afternoon. Ryan flew out of Newark around the same time. Larry Sr.'s mother, sister, brother-in-law, and brother were driving down to Orlando, where they would stay with a relative and eventually meet with my sons. My prayers were still sprinkled with anxiety, but God's peace overruled my fears. Surely the Lord was assuring me that they would all be with him soon.

At 11:30 a.m. on Thursday, February 1, I received a phone call from Ryan.

"Mom," he began.

"Yes, what is it?" I asked, holding my breath for a second. Why was he calling?

"I just landed and received a phone call from Uncle Tim," he reported softly. "Dad died early this morning, before we could get to him."

I couldn't believe what I was hearing.

"What, what did you say?"

"Dad died this morning," he repeated.

"Oh, no! Oh, no!" I cried.

"I have to go now, Mom, I'll call you later. Larry is about to land." He hung up.

I felt weak. My knees buckled. I leaned against the wall of the kitchen to brace myself. I felt light-headed. My heart was racing; my breathing took effort. *How could this be happening? What about my prayers? Why did God let this happen? They were all on their way!*

I cried openly. I complained to my mother.

"Why weren't my prayers answered? How will we know if he gave his heart back to the Lord?"

Before I could speak another word, I was interrupted by my three-year-old granddaughter. I had forgotten she was sitting at the kitchen table, coloring.

"Grandma?" she asked.

"What is it, Sweetheart?"

She tilted her head, hesitated, then looked at me with her big, blue eyes and asked, "Is Jesus in trouble?"

Her words pierced me. "Is Jesus in trouble?" She could hear the disappointment and anger in my voice.

"No, Honey," I replied. "Jesus isn't in trouble. Everything is okay!" I didn't want her to know the truth of how angry I was with the Lord for not answering my prayers the way I'd wanted.

An hour later, Larry Jr. called. He had heard the sad news. What we didn't know was that my ex-husband had a blood clot in the right ventricle of his heart. He had been told by the doctor that he could go at any time, but he never shared that with my son in their conversations. Now the pieces of the puzzle began to fit together. Everyone could see that it was not meant to be that anyone would be with Larry before his death. Not even the hospice chaplain spoke to him as he had intended. The last hours of his life were reserved for just he and God. The Holy Spirit had chased him down to Miami until it was only the two of them. How great was the love of God to bring him to that point of decision! How wide was God's mercy! How plentiful His grace!

The next day, Larry Jr. called again.

"Mom, I can see the mercy of God everywhere. The hospice workers said that Dad was their most pleasant patient. I don't know if I could have left him here if I'd come when he was alive. Where would I have taken him? The Lord was merciful to all of us."

I agreed wholeheartedly. I told Larry that the report of his father's attitude spoke to me of a changed heart. The anger and bitterness he'd carried for so many years were gone. We agreed that he had time to turn his eyes heavenward and knew the way back to God. And we had peace that he was with the Lord. The peace that only God can give at such a time.

Still reeling from the events of the past week, I awoke early on Sunday to prepare for church. After helping my granddaughters get dressed and eat breakfast, we all headed out the door to join Larry Jr.'s congregation in worship. He was still in Florida with Jen and Ryan, spending a few days together after the shock of their father's death. They needed the time to process what had happened and to comfort each other. I assured them that we would be just fine until they returned home the following Tuesday.

I knew the guest preacher well. He was the first man my son had ever ministered under as a youth pastor. He was now a retired pastor whom we loved and admired. As he began to speak, he shared that he had planned on preaching another sermon, but that "the Holy Spirit led me to Psalm 46." I was stunned. Again! How could I deny that the Lord was speaking? How could I wonder if he had everything under control?

God was speaking assurance that He knew about every detail of the events we had lived through. For a few moments, my eyes looked heavenward and I smiled. *Okay, okay, Lord! I get the message! You are*

CHAPTER 20: BE STILL—AGAIN

God and I am not! Your ways are best. You do all things well.

Jesus knows the end from the beginning. He is the Alpha and Omega. He loved me enough to reassure me over and over again that He had heard my prayers all those years, and that He had Larry in His loving hands all the time.

God's love is greater than our pain. And He allows nothing to come between Him and His children. Nothing.

* * * * * * *

INSIGHTS TO GROW BY

"But I trust in your unfailing love, my heart rejoices in your salvation" (Psalm 13:5).

Death is never easy. Whether it is someone we are close to and in a healthy relationship with, or someone we are estranged from, it still has an effect on us. Sometimes we have time to prepare for the death of someone we know and love. Although it isn't easy, we know it's inevitable. At other times, death can be sudden and unexpected, leaving unresolved issues that we have to work through. It feels wrong.

Something inside of us wants order, even in end-of-life events. Death is part of the disorder of the universe after the fall of humankind in the Garden of Eden. God warned Adam and Eve not to eat what had been forbidden. "And the Lord God commanded the man, 'You are free to eat from any tree in the garden; but you must not eat from the tree of the knowledge of good and evil, for when you eat of it you will surely die'" (Genesis 2:16-17).

Satan entered the scene and said to Eve, "You will not surely die" (Genesis 3:4). When Adam and Eve disobeyed God's command, sin entered the world along with death, and we've been suffering ever since. Death wasn't part of creation, and we weren't designed to deal with it passively. It is something that we resist on all levels—physically, emotionally and spiritually. We want to live forever. As Ecclesiastes 3:11 says, "He has also set eternity in the hearts of men." And we want those we know and love to live forever, too.

With Larry's death, I wanted the story to end in a neatly wrapped package, tied with a pretty bow, so to speak. I was sure the Lord was orchestrating the circumstances of his death so there would be reconciliation in his family relationships. Instead, there were a lot of "loose ends" and unanswered questions to work through. It wasn't how I would have planned his death.

The things I desired were good and sincere. But they weren't in the will of God. His Sovereignty—supreme power and authority—rules over our desires and wishes. Our prayers are heard by God, but he chooses to answer them in ways we often don't understand. When our family was trying to work out the details for my sons to go to his bedside, it seemed like there were delays and hindrances. We became frustrated. But looking back, we could see the hand of God working out another scenario—one we couldn't have imagined—but the best for Larry's eternal soul.

I'm sure Larry got the new life he wanted, but it wasn't here on earth. He received the new life he longed for in the presence of Jesus. God's unfailing love reached him when no one else was able to. My memory reached back to a song Larry and I used to sing together during our ministry that sums up his life. It was titled, "He Was There All the Time" (composer, Gary S. Paxton). After all his searching, Jesus was at the end of the road, waiting for Larry. God's salvation was greater than all the pain and suffering he'd endured. In the end, our prayers were answered in a way that mattered for more than the short span of this life. He was healed and restored to his Creator. And in that knowledge, we rejoiced.

CHAPTER 20: BE STILL—AGAIN

****

PRAYER

Heavenly Father, we don't pretend to understand everything about death, and why You allow circumstances to happen the way they do. But we know You are a loving and faithful God, extending Your salvation to everyone who believes that Jesus died for us and rose again to new life, giving us hope for a new life with You forever. Help us to trust You in life and in death, in joy and in sorrow, when our lives are in order and in times of confusion. We give all our unanswered questions to You, asking for Your peace to rule our hearts. In Jesus' name, Amen.

CHAPTER TWENTY-ONE

IN MEMORIAM

"A father to the fatherless, a defender of widows, is God in his holy dwelling."

–Psalm 68:5

It was a beautiful, sunny day in April when we gathered at Evangel Church for a memorial service for Larry. I was surprised, but grateful, that the church had offered to host a service to remember the good that Larry had done while pastoring there.

Larry Jr. had arrived at our home the day before with his family. My joy at seeing them was overshadowed by my sadness at the occasion. My emotions fluctuated between relief that Larry was out of his suffering and with the Lord, to grief that my grandchildren would never know their grandfather. Broken families live with "how it could have been" or "how it should have been" thoughts. They were on my mind that day.

When it was time for the service, Joel and I and Larry and his family rode to the church where Ryan and other family members had already gathered. I carefully placed a piece of poster board on an easel in the foyer that I'd filled with photos of Larry's life—from a Revivaltime Choir record cover to our last family picture taken while he was pastoring. I chose to focus on the good in his life and not dwell on the pain of the past seventeen years.

The service began with a few remarks from the man who was presently pastoring the church. He reminded us that we were there to hold Larry's years of ministry in honor and esteem. He recalled that Larry spoke of eternal things when he pastored, knowing that lives were held in the balance, sharing how people were touched by his ministry and how many came to the Lord under his preaching. Then he looked directly at my sons and told them the church was grateful for their father's ministry there.

I was humbled by his inclusion of me in his remarks, recognizing the contributions I'd made as a pastor's wife.

By the time the pastor concluded, I was crying. I knew it would be difficult to maintain my composure with my emotions so raw, so I sent up a silent prayer, asking the Lord to help me and give me His grace for the hour. He did.

Ryan was the first to share about his dad. He picked up a box of tissues on his way up to the podium and spoke.

"Thank you, everybody, for coming. Thank you for the cards, emails, phone calls, and text messages. The day after my dad passed away, I received one hundred and forty emails from friends and family."

Ryan choked back tears. Seeing him grieve made my heart pound. I lowered my head to catch my tears in my tissue. After taking a deep breath, I looked up and listened. My son was exhibiting enormous courage, and I was proud of him.

"I remember one email in particular. It read, 'you'll never forget the feeling of sorrow that you feel now. But the void will be filled with memories of your father.'"

He spoke to an audience of around seventy. I glanced over my shoulder to see faces from past and present relationships. My heart echoed his gratitude. *Thank You, Lord, that all these people were willing to come to this service and show their support.*

Ryan continued.

"My dad was always willing to try new things, even if he knew he wasn't able to do it. He wasn't athletic, but he came to all my Little League practices because he wanted to participate. He watched me play.

He had a sense of humor and always found something beautiful in others. He used to make us watch the Miss America pageant with him, finding something beautiful about each contestant.

My dad found beauty in nature and had a passion for growing plants and flowers. He knew they had to be in the proper environment to grow. He brought that passion into his ministry. At each baby dedication service he conducted, he gave a letter to the child, admonishing them to keep themselves in the church environment."

Ryan spoke of his father's caring nature, and how he wanted to bring good experiences to his family and to those he ministered to.

I have a lot of memories of my dad. The first is that he was very tall to me as a boy. I used to think 'My dad can beat up your dad!' There are other memories, but the memory that will always be etched in my mind is that of him standing in this pulpit preaching, and of him singing with my mom, 'It Is Well With My Soul.' Despite everything that happened, I can say, it is well with my soul."

Tears flowed once again. My gratitude to the Lord for hearing my cries so many years prior overwhelmed me. To hear my son honoring his father, instead of feeling bitter towards him, was humbling.

When Ryan was through, Larry Jr. walked to the platform, looked out over the crowd, and read a letter he'd written to his father.

He stood confidently and spoke as he'd done so many times from behind a pulpit.

"Dear Dad, I'm writing to you because I have questions. Many unanswered questions that you left behind. The kinds of questions for which I don't expect to receive any answers—only the benefit of asking them. There seems to be something I need, not in the answers but in the asking.

One question that I don't have, concerns where you are now. I don't need to ask that, because of what Jesus said in John 10:28. He said that those who belong to Him are given 'eternal life, and they shall never perish; no one can snatch them out of my hand.' Dad, I know to whom you belong, I know this because I saw you with my own eyes. Like most young boys, you were my hero. I knew what was important to you. I grew to understand that your faith was real. I remember that your ministry was real."

We all listened intently to what Larry shared.

He went on to say that as a boy, he listened to his father's sermons and knew he was authentic and sincere. He recalled how his father spoke about the Old Testament character named Joseph, and how his painful life had been redeemed by God. Eventually, all the suffering of Joseph's life was worked out for his good, and nothing separated him from the God who loved him.

Larry Jr. questioned whether his father would have wanted him to follow in his footsteps of pastoral ministry.

"Dad, were you aware that God had called and gifted me, too, to speak into the lives and hearts of others about their relationship with Jesus?"

Larry recounted the conversation they had when he was a teenager on what he would do with his life. When he told his dad that he wanted to be in ministry, he could see the pain in his father's face. He knew he wouldn't want him to go through what he'd experienced. In the letter, he asked his father if he knew his son was watching and listening when he became frustrated, when conflicts arose in the church, when he felt rejected.

Then he continued.

"Things became difficult, more difficult than perhaps you had ever imagined. And so you questioned your calling... and eventually you questioned your very identity. It seemed as though you no longer believed things were being worked out for your good. And so you decided to change things yourself: you left your ministry; you left your family; you left behind the person I knew you to be.

You began wondering...searching...one moment thinking you had found what you were looking for...the next moment changing direction. That cycle repeated so many times, and each time I hoped you would change direction to head back home. What were you looking for? How would you even be able to know when you found it?

I'm sorry that you wandered so far. When I saw you walk out the front door of our home, I never expected we would be thousands of miles apart some day. But apparently that is how far away you needed to go.

[In Miami you became] immobilized and destitute, surrounded by drug addicts and thieves, completely dependent on the compassion of strangers to make life last a few more days. Did you know I would never have let you stay there? Did you know that if I had made it down there in time, I wouldn't have left you in that place? That I couldn't have? Were you surprised that I called you there every day? Did you think I had forgotten

about you in just a few months' time? Did you think you were worthless? Or unforgivable? Or unlovable?"

My tears kept flowing. I wasn't the only one. Everyone around me was crying at the thoughts Larry Jr. was sharing. He was expressing what we all knew to be true. That no one, no matter how far they wander from God, is without value and worth. God's relentless love will chase them to a place of surrender.

I was running out of tissues, but it didn't matter. My son was sharing from his heart and bringing healing to us all. His questions were our questions.

Larry Jr. shared that he learned a great lesson from his experience. He learned that ultimately God is in control, and we are not. He had spent the first half of his life trying to be like his father, and the second half trying to be as different from him as possible. In his pursuit of his own identity, he learned that when a void appears in our hearts, it is because God Himself is planning to fill the space. I love the quote he referred to at this point in his sharing: "Sometimes God allows what he hates in order to accomplish what he loves." (Joni Eareckson Tada, *The God I Love: A Lifetime of Walking with Jesus*, Zondervan, 2003) I knew it was true for all of us. God had filled the void left in our hearts with Himself. There is no greater love than God's divine love!

My son shared that on the last night when he tried to call his father—without getting through—he believes his father finally found the peace he'd searched for and the love he'd longed for. He believed that in the silence of his hospice room, God reminded Larry of His relentless, inescapable love, and that he still belonged to Jesus. No matter how far his father wandered, it was never too far in the end.

Larry ended with these words:

"I'm grateful that you've finally found what you were searching for: you've found peace and rest. I just want you to

know that I've found it too, only on this side of eternity. Back here, where the questions are, and where God's peace is found less in the answers than in the asking."

Silence filled the sanctuary as we contemplated these last words. They were powerful words, poignant and comforting at the same time.

At that point, we all stood and sang the hymn, "It Is Well With My Soul." The words were penned by Horatio Spafford, a successful lawyer whose home in Chicago was destroyed by fire in 1871. He sent his wife and four daughters to England while their home was being rebuilt. While crossing the Atlantic, the ship sank. His wife wired him from England saying, "Saved Alone." Spafford boarded a ship to retrieve his wife, asking the ship's captain to notify him when the ship passed the spot where his daughters had died. The captain knocked on his door, and Spafford went to the deck of the ship and penned the words to the hymn:

> When peace, like a river, attendeth my way,
> When sorrows like sea billows roll
> Whatever my lot, Thou has taught me to say,
> It is well with my soul.
>
> Tho' Satan should buffet, tho' trials should come,
> Let this blest assurance control,
> That Christ hath regarded my helpless estate,
> And shed His own blood for my soul.
>
> And, Lord, haste the day when my faith shall be sight,
> The clouds be rolled back as a scroll:
> The trump shall resound and the Lord shall descend,
> "Even so"—it is well with my soul.
> Chorus: It is well with my soul, it is well, it is well with my soul.
> (Horatio Spafford, 1828-1888)

As I sang, tears cascaded down my face. There were a few times when I thought I would lose control and sob. But as I silently prayed, the Lord gave me the strength I needed.

After the service, my sons and I hugged. I still cried, but my tears were from the uncontainable joy I felt. To see my sons still walking with the Lord and hear them expose their tender hearts, sharing what they'd learned through our experience, was overwhelming. My joy was only matched by my gratitude.

****

INSIGHTS TO GROW BY

"I write to you, young men, because you are strong, and the word of God lives in you, and you have overcome the evil one" (1 John 2:14).

When their father left, my sons could have taken many roads. Their hearts were crushed, as was mine. It would have been easy to make choices that had not only negative temporal consequences, but also negative eternal consequences.

As I was making my way through a deluge of decisions that had to be made, Ryan and Larry Jr. were also struggling through their own feelings and reactions to what had happened. However, they weren't alone in the choices they needed to make.

The men of my home church surrounded them. My brother immediately filled the void left by Larry's abandonment. The youth pastor mentored Ryan and stayed in touch with Larry Jr. while he was in college. My brother came to our house regularly and showed Ryan how to do "guy" things, like work on his car and repair things around the house. He took him fishing and strengthened the bond that had already been established in his childhood.

Other men in the church made an effort to stay connected to my sons. They helped ensure their needs were met so they could get a college education. Larry and Ryan worked while they were in school and took out student loans. But the church also helped.

For example, the church gave Ryan a financial gift when he enrolled for his freshman year at a Christian college in a neighboring state. Not long after he received that generous gift, I asked the person who initiated help for Ryan why it had been done. His response was godly and filled with grace. He told me that he was helping Ryan out of a sense of responsibility to take care of him and see that he was able to have a future, in spite of what had happened.

These men took the opportunity to show God's love to my sons. They were embraced and reassured that the love of their Heavenly Father, demonstrated through the actions of these men, would always be theirs, and that God would continue to provide for them. It was a risk the men took, not knowing if their investment of time and energy would have positive results, but they took it anyway. I'm grateful for their investment and for the return they received. They could have thrust shame onto my sons because of the choices their father made, but instead they drenched them in love.

First Corinthians 13:8 says, "Love never fails." This passage is speaking of God's "agape" or perfect love. His kind of love is hard to resist when it is shown by the body of Christ to those who are reeling from personal tragedy or disaster. It could be the difference between staying in the church, hearing God's life-giving Word to overcome the evil one, or turning from the church and wandering through life without hope—or worse—with a bitter heart.

The church of Jesus Christ is offered opportunities to show the love of God in tangible ways to those who are hurting. Peter writes in his first book, "Finally, all of you, live in harmony with one another; be sympathetic, love as brothers, be compassionate and humble" (1 Peter 3:8). And in 1 John 3:17 we read, "If anyone has material possessions and sees his brother in need but has no pity on him, how can the love of God be in him?"

I have heard of other families in similar circumstances to mine where the wives and children were rejected by their church after being abandoned by their husband and father; this only added to their pain. I believe God would have us make the choice to love unconditionally, allowing His divine love to flow through us. Eternity will reveal the difference it has made in someone's life.

****

PRAYER

Lord, help us to love others without reservation. Give us the wisdom and courage to reach out to those who are suffering. Open our eyes to see beyond the hurt and anger and into a heart that is breaking. Remind us that our words and actions matter, and that we can make a difference in the life of someone who is in pain. Strengthen us as we follow You and obey Your command to love as You have loved us. In Jesus' name and for His sake, Amen.

CHAPTER TWENTY-TWO

"TO GIVE YOU HOPE AND A FUTURE"

"We are hard pressed on every side, but not crushed; perplexed, but not in despair; persecuted, but not abandoned; struck down, but not destroyed."

–2 Corinthians 4:8

As I walked down the corridor of the church to the fellowship hall, I could smell the aroma of freshly prepared food. The leader of the women's ministry had invited me to speak at a luncheon, and anticipation filled my heart. I slowly walked toward the open door. The room was beautifully decorated, with a flower arrangement centered on each table. Several women bustled around with last minute preparations. The attention to detail was obvious, convincing me that this gathering was important to the leadership. I felt privileged to be there as their speaker.

After a briefing on the order of events, the leaders invited me to pray with them for our time together. The fellowship hall was soon filled with women. They greeted each other with a hug or kiss and were obviously as excited as I was to be there. We enjoyed our meal, and then I was introduced. I'd chosen the title of "New Beginnings" for what the Lord had placed on my heart and based it on Jeremiah 29:11—"to give you hope and a future." There had been many opportunities to share my testimony over the past few years. But I didn't expect what was about to happen.

As I shared my story, I came to the point where I told how I'd been abandoned by my husband, and that he'd left me for a man. The words hadn't completely left my lips when a woman sitting to my right began to wail and sob into her hands. Startled, we all turned toward her. A couple of women sitting next to her placed their hands on her shoulders in an attempt to comfort her. When she caught her breath, she blurted, "I thought I was the only one!"

She, too, had been abandoned by her husband and was carrying the shame of her circumstances. She thought she was alone in her suffering. Truthfully, we are two of many women who've been abandoned by our husbands for a man. Over the years, I've encountered women who were the wives of pastors, church leaders, college professors, and church goers who have lived through similar horror in their marriages. There have also been men who watched their wives leave them for a woman, tearing their families apart as their hearts were broken.

That day at the luncheon, I joined the other women to comfort this woman who felt so alone in her pain. I prayed aloud for her: "Lord, hear the cries of Your daughter. Please heal her broken heart, as You've done for me. Help her to overcome the pain of betrayal and rejection. Remove the shame she feels. Send Your Holy Spirit to comfort her and give her a new beginning. And we will praise You for Your goodness and mercy in her life. Thank You, Father, that we are never alone."

Similar prayers have been offered for those who have been abandoned, in an effort to reassure them that although the one they loved left, the One who loves them most will never leave. I pray that they too will discover, "*He Left*, but *God Stayed*."

CHAPTER 22: "TO GIVE YOU HOPE AND A FUTURE"

* * * * * * *

INSIGHTS TO GROW BY

"I will give you the treasures of darkness, riches stored in secret places, so that you may know that I am the Lord, the God of Israel, who summons you by name" (Isaiah 45:3).

I'm reminded of something Helen Keller said. "All the world is full of suffering. It is also full of overcoming."

Helen was born a healthy child and began to speak by the age of one. But at the age of two, she suffered from an illness that rendered her blind, deaf, and mute. The rest of her life was spent in overcoming these difficulties. She learned to communicate through sign language and eventually became the first deaf and blind person to graduate from Radcliffe University. As an adult, she became an educator and humanitarian, traveling and speaking in thirty-nine countries until her death in 1968 at the age of eighty-eight.

Why am I sharing this with you in the last chapter? Because I've come to understand that all of us have something to overcome in life. We *all* face trials, hardships, abuses, and betrayals that could destroy us, if we let them. If we live long enough, our hearts will be broken—perhaps many times. And when our hearts are broken, it is easy to give up in despair. But we don't need to be destroyed by the things that happen to us.

We *can* overcome through the power and grace of God! The Lord promises to give us a future that is filled with His presence and blessing, no matter what our past has done to us. We can overcome.

In the book of Revelation, the Holy Spirit addresses seven churches. The messages to these churches came through a vision given to John. Over and over again he repeats, "To him who overcomes." Each church is commended for their good deeds but also urged to repent of their sin. Then the Lord Jesus promises that to him who overcomes, He will give the right to sit with Him on His throne, "just as I overcame and sat down with my Father on his throne" (Revelation 3:21).

The word for *overcome* in Greek, *nikao*, means "to conquer, prevail, and get the victory." When Jesus rose from the dead, He was completely victorious over sin, death and every evil force in the universe. He prevailed and conquered our enemy! Because we belong to Him and His Spirit lives in us, we too can be victorious over all the things we face in life. Romans 8:11 confirms this truth: "And if the Spirit of him who raised Jesus from the dead is living in you, he who raised Christ from the dead will also give life to your mortal bodies through the Spirit, who lives in you."

The same Spirit who raised Christ from the dead is living in us! That's an overwhelming statement. On most days, if you're like me, you don't feel the power of God surging through your veins. But the promise is that God lives in us, and by His power we will be victorious, just as Jesus was by His obedience and the work He accomplished on the cross. His power in us is enough.

To this day, I can still hear the voice of my mother telling me to be an overcomer. Whatever I was experiencing, she encouraged me to overcome the problem or rise above the person that was causing me pain. The lesson I learned early in life prepared me for the seasons of life that had the potential to destroy me. Overcoming doesn't mean ignoring the pain. That's called denial. It does mean rising above it. It doesn't mean allowing others to repeatedly wound us, but forgiving offenses and moving forward, giving the Holy Spirit room to work on our behalf.

Looking back over my life, I can see the grace of God carrying me through the pain, enabling me to overcome. God showed up in so many tangible ways. He especially used the church and fellow Christians to demonstrate His love and grace to me and my sons. This story could have had a different ending. It could have ended in tragedy from the crushing blows that we were dealt. We could have been ostracized and rejected by our church. They could have chosen to judge my family for what Larry did to us and to them.

Instead, the church rose to meet the challenge of being the hands and feet--and the heart--of Jesus. We were lovingly embraced, surrounded, and ministered to in our suffering. God's love and grace shone through the darkness in more ways than I've been able to share in this book. How much more painful our experience would have been if the church hadn't risen to the opportunity to help pick up the broken pieces of our lives. I cherish the dear people who were there for us.

Perhaps your experience has been different. Maybe during your darkest hours, those who you depended on turned their backs on you. Maybe you're living in the hell of abandonment by your friends, family or church. Let me assure you that their actions don't represent the character of God—they don't represent who He is. He longs to ease our suffering through people who exhibit His compassion and tender loving care. He wants to speak into our lives through those who are spiritually sensitive and listen to His voice. If you aren't in a church that is helping to heal your wounds, find a church that will. You don't have to walk this path alone!

I have learned that there are treasures to be discovered in the darkness. Things like surrender and trust. Things like praising through the pain. Things like the character of God and a deeper knowledge of who He is-- a greater understanding of His love and faithfulness. These are riches that we learn in the secret places of suffering. Riches that can't be bought. Lessons that stay with us for the rest of our lives and can't be stolen. They're embedded in our hearts, written by the very hand of God.

The truth I've testified to in these chapters is that God will not abandon you. Be on the lookout for His grace in your life. Don't believe for one moment that your circumstances are too difficult for

Him, or that He's unaware of what you're going through. God sees and records each tear. He suffers with you. He is carrying you in His arms and will never let you go. Isaiah 40:11 says: "He tends his flock like a shepherd; He gathers the lambs in his arms and carries them close to his heart; he gently leads those that have young." Can you feel His loving arms around you? Can you sense His peace reassuring you that you will come out on the other side? You will be victorious because of His unending and unfailing love for you! "For the Lord your God is the one who goes with you to fight for you against your enemies to give you victory" (Deuteronomy 20:4).

Go into your future with confidence in God's power to make your dreams come true. He will help you reach your fullest potential. God can transform your anger into energy, helping you to act in constructive ways to reach your goals. I know that if you surrender everything to the Lover of your soul, you will be amazed at the results. I know this is true, because this is what He has done in and through me. And He will do it for you!

I've done my best to serve the Lord—even in my brokenness. Act on your strengths, not on your weaknesses. Appreciate the gifts, talents, and abilities that God has given you. Always trust that He will give you whatever you need to do His will. Move forward in His favor. As we see God working through us, together we will be able to say: "Shouts of joy and victory resound in the tents of the righteous; 'The Lord's right hand has done mighty things! The Lord's right hand is lifted high; the Lord's right hand has done mighty things!'" (Psalm 118:15-16).

Believe it, live in it, rest in it, and you will become all He created you to be!

CHAPTER 22: "TO GIVE YOU HOPE AND A FUTURE"

****

PRAYER

Dear Lord, I pray now for everyone who has read this book. I pray that You will reveal Yourself to them, and that they will come to know You as their loving, faithful Father. I pray that You will help them to walk on the path that You've set before them, growing into strong and spiritually healthy children of the Most High God. Provide all they need to accomplish Your purpose in their lives and bring glory to Your name. May they stand amazed in Your presence every day of their lives and enjoy You forever in heaven. In Jesus' name and for His glory, Amen.

COMFORT AND ENCOURAGEMENT FROM THE PSALMS

1:6 – For the Lord watches over the way of the righteous.

3:3-4 – But you are a shield around me, O Lord; you bestow glory on me and lift up my head. To the Lord I cry aloud, and he answers me from his holy hill.

3:5 – I lie down and sleep; I wake again, because the Lord sustains me.

4:3 – Know that the Lord set apart the godly for himself: the Lord will hear when I call to him.

4:8 – I will lie down and sleep in peace, for you alone, O Lord, make me dwell in safety.

5:3 – In the morning, O Lord, you hear my voice; in the morning I lay my requests before you, and wait in expectation.

5:12 – For surely, O Lord, you bless the righteous; you surround them with your favor as with a shield.

6:4 – Turn, O Lord, and deliver me; save me because of your unfailing love.

8:1-2 – O Lord, our Lord, how majestic is your name in all the earth! You have set your glory above the heavens. From the lips of children and infants you have ordained praise.

9:9-10 – The Lord is a refuge for the oppressed, a stronghold in times of trouble. Those who know your name will trust in you, for you, Lord, have never forsaken those who seek you.

10:14 – But you, O God, do see trouble and grief; you consider it to take it in hand. The victim commits himself to you; you are the helper of the fatherless.

13:5-6 – But I trust in your unfailing love; my heart rejoices in your salvation. I will sing to the Lord, for he has been good to me.

16:5-6, 8, 11 – Lord, you have assigned me my portion and my cup; you have made my lot secure. The boundary lines have fallen for me in pleasant places; surely I have a delightful inheritance. I have set the Lord always before me. Because he is at my right hand, I will not be shaken. You have made known to me the path of life; you will fill me with joy in your presence, with eternal pleasure at your right hand.

17:6-7 – I call on you, O God, for you will answer me; give ear to me and hear my prayer. Show the wonder of your great love, you who save by your right hand those who take refuge in you from their foes.

18:1-3 – I love you, O Lord, my strength. The Lord is my rock, in whom I take refuge. He is my shield and the horn of my salvation, my stronghold. I call to the Lord, who is worthy of praise, and I am saved from my enemies.

18:25-33 – To the faithful you show yourself faithful, to the blameless you show yourself blameless, to the pure you show yourself pure, but to the crooked you show yourself shrewd. You save the humble but bring low those whose eyes are haughty. You, O Lord, keep my lamp burning; my God turns my darkness into light. With your help I can advance against a troop; with my God I can scale a wall. As for God, his way is perfect; the word of the Lord is flawless. He is a shield for all who take refuge in him. For who is God besides the Lord? And who is the Rock except our God? It is God who arms me with strength and makes my way perfect. He makes my feet like the feet of a deer; he enables me to stand on the heights.

20:7 – Some trust in chariots and some in horses, but we trust in the name of the Lord our God.

23:4,6 – Even though I walk through the valley of the shadow of death, I will fear no evil, for you are with me. Surely goodness and love will follow me all the days of my life, and I will dwell in the house of the Lord forever.

25:1-6 – To you, O Lord, I lift up my soul; in you I trust, O my God. Do not let me be put to shame, nor let my enemies triumph over me. No one whose hope is in you will ever be put to shame, but they will be put to shame who are treacherous without excuse. Show me your ways, O Lord, teach me your paths; guide me in your truth and teach me, for you are God my Savior, and my hope is in you all day long. Remember, O Lord, your great mercy and love, for they are from of old.

25:20-21 – Guard my life and rescue me; let me not be put to shame, for I take refuge in you. May integrity and uprightness protect me, because my hope is in you.

25:9, 10 – He guides the humble in what is right and teaches them his way. All the ways of the Lord are loving and faithful for those who keep the demands of his covenant.

27:1 – The Lord is my light and my salvation—whom shall I fear? The Lord is the stronghold of my life—of whom shall I be afraid?

27:5 – For in the day of trouble he will keep me safe in his dwelling; he will hide me in the shelter of his tabernacle and set me high upon a rock.

27:14 – Wait for the Lord; be strong and take heart and wait for the Lord.

28:7 – The Lord is my strength and my shield; my heart trusts in him, and I am helped. My heart leaps for joy and I will give thanks to him in song.

30:2, 4-5 – O Lord my God, I called to you for help and you healed me. Sing to the Lord, you saints of his; praise his holy name. For his anger lasts only a moment, but his favor lasts a lifetime; weeping may remain for a night, but rejoicing comes in the morning.

30:11 – You turned my wailing into dancing; you removed my sackcloth and clothed me with joy, that my heart may sing to you and not be silent. O Lord my God, I will give you thanks forever.

31:7, 15-16 – My times are in your hands; deliver me from my enemies and from those who pursue me. Let your face shine on your servant, save me in your unfailing love. I will be glad and rejoice in your love, for you saw my affliction and knew the anguish of my soul.

32:7-8, 10 – You are my hiding place; you will protect me from trouble and surround me with songs of deliverance. I will instruct you and teach you in the way you should go; I will counsel you and watch over you. Many are the woes of the wicked, but the Lord's unfailing love surrounds the man who trusts in him.

33:5, 18 –The Lord loves righteousness and justice; the earth is full of his unfailing love. But the eyes of the Lord are on those who fear him, on those whose hope is in his unfailing love.

33:21-22-We wait in hope for the Lord; he is our help and our shield. In him our hearts rejoice, for we trust in his holy name. May your unfailing love rest upon us, O Lord, even as we put our hope in you.

34:4-5 – I sought the Lord, and he answered me; he delivered me from all my fears. Those who look to him are radiant; their faces are never covered with shame.

34:17-19, 22 – The righteous cry out, and the Lord hears them; he delivers them from all their troubles. The Lord is close to the brokenhearted and saves those who are crushed in spirit. A righteous man may have many troubles, but the Lord delivers him from them all. The Lord redeems his servants; no one will be condemned who takes refuge in him.

36:5, 7 – Your love, O Lord, reaches to the heavens, your faithfulness to the skies. How priceless is your unfailing love! Both high and low among men find refuge in the shadow of your wings.

37: 3-7 – Trust in the Lord and do good; dwell in the land and enjoy safe pasture. Delight yourself in the Lord and he will give you the desires of your heart. Commit your way to the Lord; trust in him and he will do this: He will make your righteousness shine like the dawn, the justice of your cause like the noonday sun. Be still before the Lord and wait patiently for him. Refrain from anger and turn from wrath; do not fret—it only leads to evil.

37:23-24 – If the Lord delights in a man's way, he makes his steps firm; though he stumble, he will not fall, for the Lord upholds him with his hand.

37:39-40 – The salvation of the righteous comes from the Lord; he is their stronghold in time of trouble. The Lord helps them and delivers them; he delivers them from the wicked and saves them, because they take refuge in him.

40:1-3 – I waited patiently for the Lord; he turned to me and heard my cry. He lifted me out of the slimy pit, out of the mud and mire; he set my feet on a rock and gave me a firm place to stand. He put a new song in my mouth, a hymn of praise to our God.

40:11 – Do not withhold your mercy from me, O Lord; may your love and your truth always protect me.

42:5, 8 – Why so downcast, O my soul? Why so disturbed within me? Put your hope in God, for I will yet praise him, my Savior and my God. By day the Lord directs his love, at night his song is with me—a prayer to the God of my life.

44:26 – Rise up and help us; redeem us because of your unfailing love.

46:1- God is our refuge and strength, an ever-present help in trouble.

46:10 – Be still, and know that I am God; I will be exalted among the nations, I will be exalted in the earth.

51:1 – Have mercy on me, O God, according to your unfailing love; according to your great compassion blot out my transgressions.

51:17 – The sacrifices of God are a broken spirit; a broken and contrite heart, O God, you will not despise.

52:8 – But I am like an olive tree flourishing in the house of God; I trust in God's unfailing love for ever and ever.

55:16-17, 22 – But I call to God, and the Lord saves me. Evening, morning and noon I cry out in distress, and he hears my voice. Cast your cares on the Lord and he will sustain you; he will never let the righteous fall.

56:3-4 – When I am afraid, I will trust in you. In God, whose word I praise, in God I trust; I will not be afraid. What can mortal man do to me?

57:10 – For great is your love, reaching to the heavens; your faithfulness reaches to the skies.

59:16 – But I will sing of your strength, in the morning I will sing of your love; for you are my fortress, my refuge in times of trouble.

60:5, 12 – Save us and help us with your right hand, that those you love may be delivered. With God we will gain the victory, and he will trample down our enemies.

62:5, 8 – Find rest, O my soul, in God alone; my hope comes from him. Trust in him at all times, O people; pour out your hearts to him, for God is our refuge.

63:3 – Because your love is better than life, my lips will glorify you.

66:20 – Praise be to God, who has not rejected my prayer or withheld his love from me!

69:16 – Answer me, O Lord, out of the goodness of your love; in your great mercy turn to me.

71:1-3 – In you, O Lord, I have taken refuge; let me never be put to shame. Rescue me and deliver me in your righteousness; turn your ear to me and save me. Be my rock of refuge, to which I can always go; give the command to save me, for you are my rock and my fortress.

71:20-21- Though you have made me see troubles, many and bitter, you will restore my life again; from the depths of the earth you will again bring me up. You will increase my honor and comfort me once again.

85:7 – Show us your unfailing love, O Lord, and grant us your salvation.

86:5-7 – You are forgiving and good, O Lord, abounding in love to all who call to you. Hear my prayer, O Lord; listen to my cry for mercy. In the day of trouble I will call to you, for you will answer me.

86:11-13, 15 – Teach me your way, O Lord, and I will walk in your truth; give me an undivided heart, that I may fear your name. I will praise you, O Lord my God, with all my heart; I will glorify your name forever. For great is your love toward me; you have delivered me from the depths of the grave. But you, O Lord, are a compassionate and gracious God, slow to anger, abounding in love and faithfulness.

89:2 – I will declare that your love stands firm forever, that you established your faithfulness in heaven itself.

90:14 – Satisfy us in the morning with your unfailing love, that we may sing for joy and be glad all our days.

91:1-2 ,11 – He who dwells in the shelter of the Most High will rest in the shadow of the Almighty. I will say of the Lord, "He is my refuge and my fortress, my God, in whom I trust." For he will command his angels concerning you, to guard you in all your ways.

94:12-14 – Blessed is the man you discipline, O Lord, the man you teach from your law; you grant him relief from days of trouble, till a pit is dug for the wicked. For the Lord will not reject his people; he will never forsake his inheritance.

94:18-19 –When I said, "My foot is slipping," your love, O Lord, supported me. When anxiety was great within me, your consolation brought joy to my soul.

100:5 – For the Lord is good and his love endures forever; his faithfulness continues through all generations.

103:4 – [The Lord] redeems your life from the pit and crowns you with love and compassion.

103:8, 10-11, 13 - The Lord is compassionate and gracious, slow to anger, abounding in love. He does not treat us as our sins deserve or repay us according to our iniquities. For as high as the heavens are above the earth, so great is his love for those who fear him. As a father has compassion on his children, so the Lord has compassion on those who fear him.

107:1 – Give thanks to the Lord, for he is good; his love endures forever.

108:4-6 – For great is your love, higher than the heavens; your faithfulness reaches to the skies. Be exalted, O God, above the heavens and let your glory be over all the earth. Save us and help us with your right hand, that those you love may be delivered.

109:26 – Help me, O Lord my God; save me in accordance with your love.

111:10 – The fear of the Lord is the beginning of wisdom; all who follow his precepts have good understanding. To him belongs eternal praise.

112: 1, 7 – Praise the Lord. Blessed is the man who fears the Lord, who finds great delight in his commands. He will have no fear of bad news; his heart is steadfast, trusting in the Lord. His heart is secure, he will have no fear; in the end he will look in triumph on his foes.

115:1 – Not to us, O Lord, not to us but to your name be the glory, because of your love and faithfulness.

116:5-7 – The Lord is gracious and righteous; our God is full of compassion. The Lord protects the simple-hearted; when I was in great need, he saved me. Be at rest once more, O my soul, for the Lord has been good to you.

117:1-2 – Praise the Lord, all you nations; extol him, all you people. For great is his love toward us, and the faithfulness of the Lord endures forever.

118:1, 6-8 – Give thanks to the Lord, for he is good; his love endures forever. The Lord is with me; I will not be afraid. What can man do to me? The Lord is with me; he is my helper. I will look in triumph on my enemies. It is better to take refuge in the Lord than to trust in man.

119:76, 88 – May your unfailing love be my comfort, according to your promise to your servant. Preserve my life according to your love, and I will obey the statutes of your mouth.

121:1-8 – I lift up my eyes to the hills—where does my help come from? My help comes from the Lord, the Maker of heaven and earth. He will not let your foot slip—he who watches over you will not slumber; indeed, he who watches over Israel will neither slumber nor sleep. The Lord watches over you—the Lord is your shade at your right hand; the sun will not harm you by day, nor the moon by night. The Lord will keep you from all harm—he will watch over your life; the Lord will watch over your coming and going both now and forevermore.

130:7 – O Israel, put your hope in the Lord, for with the Lord is unfailing love and with him is full redemption.

135:13-14 – Your name, O Lord, endures forever, your renown, O Lord, through all generations. For the Lord will vindicate his people and have compassion on his servants.

136:1-3 – Give thanks to the Lord, for he is good. His love endures forever. Give thanks to the God of gods. His love endures forever. Give thanks to the Lord of lords. His love endures forever.

138:2-3 – I will bow down toward your holy temple and will praise your name for your love and your faithfulness, for you have exalted above all things your name and your word. When I called, you answered me; you made me bold and stouthearted.

138: 8 – The Lord will fulfill his purpose for me; your love, O Lord, endures forever—do not abandon the works of your hands.

139:11-12 – If I say, "Surely the darkness will hide me and the light become night around me," even the darkness will not be dark to you; the night will shine like the day, for darkness is as light to you.

143:8, 12 – Let the morning bring me word of your unfailing love, for I have put my trust in you. In your unfailing love, silence my enemies; destroy all my foes, for I am your servant.

145:8, 14-20 – The Lord is gracious and compassionate, slow to anger and rich in love. The Lord upholds all those who fall and lifts up all who are bowed down. The eyes of all look to you, and you give them their food at the proper time. You open your hand and satisfy the desires of every living thing. The Lord is righteous in all his ways and loving toward all he has made. The Lord is near to all who call on him, to all who call on him in truth. He fulfills the desires of those who fear him; he hears their cry and saves them. The Lord watches over all who love him, but all the wicked he will destroy.

147:3 – He heals the brokenhearted and binds up their wounds.

147:11 –The Lord delights in those who fear him, who put their hope in his unfailing love.

ASSURANCE OF GOD'S LOVE

OLD TESTAMENT

EXODUS

15:13 – In your unfailing love you will lead the people you have redeemed. In your strength you will guide them to your holy dwelling.

20:6 – But showing love to a thousand generations of those who love me and keep my commandments.

34:6-7 – The Lord, the Lord, the compassionate and gracious God, slow to anger, abounding in love and faithfulness, maintaining love to thousands, and forgiving wickedness, rebellion and sin.

I KINGS

8:22 – O Lord, God of Israel, there is no God like you in heaven above or on earth below—you who keep your covenant of love with your servants who continue wholeheartedly in your way.

I CHRONICLES

16:34 – Give thanks to the Lord, for he is good; his love endures forever.

ISAIAH

38:17 – In your love you kept me from the pit of destruction; you have put all my sins behind your back.

54:10 – Though the mountains be shaken and the hills be removed, yet my unfailing love for you will not be shaken nor my covenant of peace be removed, says the Lord, who has compassion on you.

JEREMIAH

31:3 – I have loved you with an everlasting love; I have drawn you with loving-kindness.

LAMENTATIONS

3:22-24 - Because of the Lord's great love we are not consumed, for his compassions never fail. They are new every morning; great is your faithfulness. I say to myself, "The Lord is my portion; therefore I will wait for him."

ZEPHANIAH

3:17 – The Lord your God is with you, he is mighty to save. He will take great delight in you, he will quiet you with his love, he will rejoice over you with singing.

NEW TESTAMENT

JOHN

3:16 – For God so loved the world that he gave his one and only son, that whoever believes in him shall not perish but have eternal life.

14:21, 23 – Whoever has my commands and obeys them, he is the one who loves me. He who loves me will be loved by my Father, and I too will love him and show myself to him. If anyone loves me, he will obey my teaching. My Father will love him, and we will come to him and make our home with him.

15:9 – As the Father has loved me, so have I loved you. Now remain in my love.

17:23 – I in them and you in me. May they be brought to complete unity to let the world know that you sent me and have loved them even as you have loved me.

ROMANS

5:5, 8 – And hope does not disappoint us, because God has poured out his love into our hearts by the Holy Spirit, whom he has given us. But God demonstrates his own love for us in this: While we were still sinners, Christ died for us.

8:35-39 – Who shall separate us from the love of Christ? Shall trouble or hardship or persecution or famine or nakedness or danger or sword? As it is written: "For your sake we face death all day long; we are considered as sheep to be slaughtered." No, in all these things we are more than conquerors through him who loved us. For I am convinced that neither death nor life, neither angels nor demons, neither the present nor the future, nor any powers, neither height nor depth, nor anything in all creation, will be able to separate us from the love of God that is in Christ Jesus our Lord.

GALATIANS

2:20 – I have been crucified with Christ and I no longer live, but Christ lives in me. The life I live in the body, I live by faith in the Son of God, who loved me and gave himself for me.

EPHESIANS

1:4-5 – For he chose us in him before the creation of the world to be holy and blameless in his sight. In love he predestined us to be adopted as his sons through Jesus Christ, in accordance with his pleasure and will.

2:4 – But because of his great love for us, God, who is rich in mercy, made us alive with Christ even when we were dead in transgressions—it is by grace you have been saved.

3:17-19 – So that Christ may dwell in your hearts through faith. And I pray that you, being rooted and established in love, may have power together with all the saints, to grasp how wide and long and high and deep is the love of Christ, and to know this love that surpasses knowledge—that you may be filled to the measure of all the fullness of God.

5:1 – Be imitators of God, therefore, as dearly loved children, and live a life of love, just as Christ loved us and gave himself up for us as a fragrant offering and sacrifice to God.

II THESSALONIANS

2:16-17 – May our Lord Jesus Christ himself and God our Father, who loved us and by his grace gave us eternal encouragement and good hope, encourage your hearts and strengthen you in every good deed and word.

TITUS

3:4 – But when the kindness and love of God our Savior appeared, he saved us, not because of righteous things we had done, but because of his mercy.

I JOHN

3:1 – How great is the love the Father has lavished on us, that we should be called the children of God! And that is what we are!

3:16 – This is how we know what love is: Jesus Christ laid down his life for us.

4:8-11 – Whoever does not love does not know God, because God is love. This is how God showed his love among us: He sent his one and only Son into the world that we might live through him. This is love: not that we loved God, but that he loved us and sent his Son as an atoning sacrifice for our sins.

4:16,19 – And so we know and rely on the love God has for us. God is love. Whoever lives in love lives in God, and God in him. We love because he first loved us.

SCRIPTURES IN BOOK BY CHAPTER:

CHAPTER 1:

Job 28:11
Psalm 55: 12-14
Psalm 55: 4-5
Psalm 94:17-19

CHAPTER 2

Jeremiah 1:5
John 3:16
Psalm 8:2,4
Psalm 27:10
Genesis 25:28
Hebrews 13:5*
Luke 1:37

CHAPTER 3

Proverbs 3:5
Proverbs 16:9
John 16:33

CHAPTER 4

Daniel 2:22
Psalm 142:6
John 10:10

CHAPTER 5

Jeremiah 29:11
I Corinthians 1:9
Psalm 46:1
Jude 24,25

CHAPTER 6

Psalm 23:4
Jeremiah 32:17
Psalm 34:18
John 16:13
John 8:32
John 14:6
Deuteronomy 33:27

CHAPTER 7

Hebrews 13:5 *
Psalm 46:10*
Psalm 63:7

CHAPTER 8

Matthew 5:4
Psalm 147:3

CHAPTER 9

Isaiah 54:5
Isaiah 54:4-6 *
Psalm 42:5
Philippians 4:19
John 17:11,15
II Thessalonians 3:3

CHAPTER 10

Ephesians 4:26-27
I John 3:20
II Corinthians 12:9
Isaiah 55:8-9

CHAPTER 11

Isaiah 30:21
Acts 2:18
Joel 2:28,29

CHAPTER 12

Genesis 1:27,31
Luke 1:26-56
Luke 8:1-3
Matthew 28:1-8
Acts 1:14
Psalm 139:14-15

CHAPTER 13

Deuteronomy 30:19
I Peter 4:4

II Corinthians 12:9 *
Deuteronomy 30:19
II Timothy 1:7
Zephaniah 3:17
Deuteronomy 30:20
II Peter 1:3-4
I Thessalonians 4:13
I Peter 5:10
Romans 8:28
II Corinthians 1:3,4

CHAPTER 14

Ephesians 3:20
Luke 12:15
Matthew 6:33
Psalm 84:11
James 1:17

CHAPTER 15

Isaiah 43:2
Proverbs 15:1
Psalm 23:3
Psalm 141:3
I Corinthians 13:4-7
Job 23:10

CHAPTER 16

II Corinthians 9:8
Isaiah 43:18,19
Johan 2:8

CHAPTER 17

Colossians 3:13
Isaiah 58:8
Matthew 6:13
John 17:14
Genesis 37-50
Genesis 50:19,20

CHAPTER 18

II Timothy 2:15
Isaiah 54:5*
Numbers 6:24-26
Joel 2:25*
Psalm 16:6

CHAPTER 19

Ecclesiastes 3:11
Song of Songs 2:10-13
Psalm 71:20
I John 4:18

CHAPTER 20

Romans 8:37-39
Psalm 46:10
Psalm 13:5
Genesis 2:16,17
Genesis 3:4
Ecclesiastes 3:11 *

CHAPTER 21

Psalm 68:5
John 10:28
I John 2:14

I Corinthians 13:8
I Peter 3:8
I John 3:17

CHAPTER 22

II Corinthians 4:8
Revelation 3:21
Romans 8:11
Deuteronomy 20:4
Isaiah 45:3
Isaiah 40:11

Verses with an asterisk (*)
are referenced in other chapters.

ABOUT THE AUTHOR

Annalee Davis, B.A., M.Div., has been published in devotionals, magazines and book compilations, including Chicken Soup for the Soul. She graduated Summa Cum Laude from New Brunswick Theological Seminary, and previously ordained in the Assemblies of God (2001), is presently ordained with the Wesleyan Church. She has served as an assistant pastor, co-pastor, pulpit supply pastor, senior pastor, and adjunct instructor at Pillar (Christian) College. She has spoken in churches and for women's retreats and conventions, and has written and taught women's Bible studies. As a Competent Communicator with Toastmasters International, she has received awards at local and area levels in New Jersey where she resides with her husband, Joel. Annalee can be reached at: rev.annalee.davis@gmail.com